ENJOYING THE
BRECON BEACONS NATIONAL PARK

ROLY SMITH

HALSGROVE

IN ASSOCIATION WITH

PARC CENEDLAETHOL BANNAU BRYCHEINIOG

50

BRECON BEACONS
NATIONAL PARK
1957–2007

First published in Great Britain in 2007

Front cover photograph: *Fan Foel, the Carmarthen Fans.*

British Library Cataloguing-in-Publication Data
A CIP record for this title is available from the British Library

ISBN 978 1 84114 645 4

HALSGROVE
Halsgrove House
Ryelands Industrial Estate, Bagley Road,
Wellington, Somerset TA21 9PZ
Tel: 01823 653777
Fax: 01823 216796
email: sales@halsgrove.com
website: www.halsgrove.com

Printed and bound by Grafiche Flaminia, Italy

Contents

Maen Llia

Special features

Map of the Area

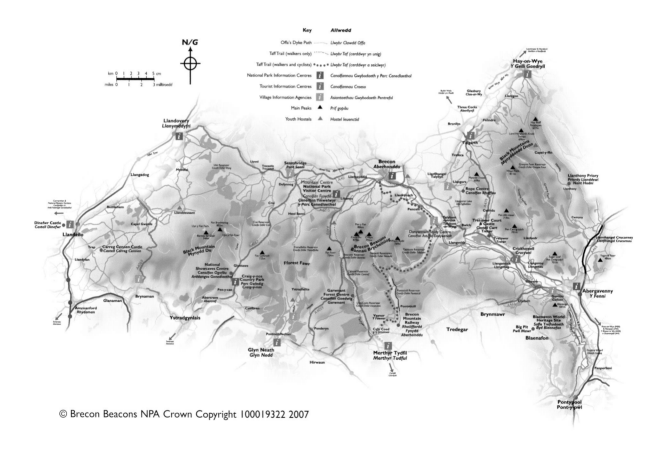

Foreword

A VERY SPECIAL PLACE

By Mary Taylor, Chairman of the Brecon Beacons National Park Authority

There's no doubting that the Brecon Beacons National Park is a very special place. It's an area that contains a stunning and diverse range of beautiful environments – from the breathtakingly steep escarpments of Pen y Fan (the highest point in Southern Britain), to picturesque reservoirs and lakes, dense forests and woodlands, wide open moors and the stunning waterfalls around Ystradfellte. We even have an internationally-designated area of geological importance within the National Park boundary. Fforest Fawr is the only UNESCO designated 'Geopark' site within a UK National Park.

But the Brecon Beacons National Park is not just about the wonderful natural environment – it is also home and a place of work for thousands of people who give the area its life, colour and heritage.

This beautiful area celebrates its 50th birthday as a National Park in 2007, and we're using the occasion to celebrate both the wonderful natural environment of the Park and the people who live and work here.

Throughout the Park's history, a delicate balance has been struck between the conservation of this beautiful and fragile environment and the needs of local communities. As we look to the Park's next 50 years, that balance needs to be maintained through careful management of the natural resources available to us.

Whatever you might look for as a visitor, you'll find something for you here. Be it a rigorous day on the hills or a few hours of pampering and fine dining at one of the local resort locations, the Brecon Beacons National Park has it all. As Chairman of the Brecon Beacons National Park Authority, you might expect me to say that, so don't just take my word for it – immerse yourself in this wonderful book and pay us a visit to find out for yourself. A visit to this beautiful landscape can re-energise, re-vitalise and refresh the mind, body and soul.

Enjoy your visit.

Pen y Fan

1. Introduction

THE BECKONING BEACONS

The branding of the UK's National Parks as "Britain's breathing spaces" was never more appropriate than in the Brecon Beacons, because the vast majority of its four million annual visitors still come from the valleys of South Wales, for whom it has been a vital lung and escape route for generations.

Since before the rapid growth and later decline of the coal mining industry, the Beacons had beckoned the people of the Rhondda and the other South Wales valleys by the striking contrast provided by their clean, fresh air and wonderful vistas to their grim everyday working conditions.

It was the proximity to the populations of these dark, industrial landscapes which was one of the major reasons for the designation of the National Park, as it was for the Peak District in northern England. Even today only 32,000 people actually live within the National Park, but its catchment area for potential day visitors runs into millions.

The Brecon Beacons are the highest ground in Britain south of Snowdonia, and form the centrepiece of the 520-square-mile (1347 sq km) National Park, designated as the tenth National Park in Britain exactly 50 years ago in 1957. It is the nearest National Park to London and the south east of England and is easily reached by train or the M4 and M50.

Brecon & Monmouthshire Canal, Talybont-on-Usk

Fan Foel, The Carmarthen Fans

With the Beacons at the centre, the National Park is bracketed by two other distinct ranges of Old Red Sandstone mountains, both confusingly described as Black. The Black Mountain (singular) or Carmarthen Fans (known as Mynydd Du in Welsh) is the real "wild west" of the Park. Here, the former royal hunting forest of Fforest Fawr contains little visited mountains such as Bannau Sir Gaer and Fan Brycheiniog, with legend-haunted lakes such as Llyn y Fan Fach sheltered beneath scree-buttressed summits.

Here also, occupying the whole of the western half of the National Park, is the Fforest Fawr Geopark, which became a member of the European Geoparks Network in 2005 for its geological heritage and a UNESCO Global Geopark in 2006. It is currently the only one in Wales. The important National Nature Reserve of Craig Cerrig-gleisiad, occupies a crag-bound hollow in the hills where rare arctic and alpine flowers bloom among the rocks, and buzzards and ravens soar overhead. Llandovery (Llanymddyfri), once an important drovers' town with a Norman castle, Llandeilo, Trecastle and Sennybridge are good centres to explore the wild west of the National Park.

The Black Mountains (plural) to the east form a natural boundary between England and Wales and were used by King Offa for his Dyke – now part of a 177-mile National Trail – during the troubled days of the Dark Ages. The chief town for the exploration of the Black Mountains is Abergavenny (Y Fenni), which is dominated by the isolated, thimble-topped hills known as Blorenge, the Sugar Loaf and Ysgyryd Fawr. Reed-fringed Llangors Lake (Llyn Syfaddan), the largest natural lake in South Wales, lies between the

Black Mountains and Brecon and is popular with all kinds of water sport enthusiasts. Its fragile eco-system has made the lake one of the Park's many Sites of Special Scientific Interest (SSSIs).

The River Wye (Afon Gwy) parallels the north west boundary of the National Park which reaches its northernmost point at the second-hand book capital of Britain, Hay-on-Wye (Y Gelli Gandryll). Dominated by its originally eleventh century castle, Hay-on-Wye is an important agricultural centre and the former cheese and butter markets are remembered in the names of its streets.

Walkers in the Central Beacons

The underlying rock of the southern part of the National Park is Millstone Grit and directly north of this is a band of limestone, creating another, totally contrasting, type of scenery which can sometimes make it feel more like the Yorkshire Dales than Wales. The twin valleys of the Mellte and Hepste rivers south of Ystradfellte have a series of magical waterfalls which enliven the well-wooded scene and perched on the edge of this delightful area is another usually unseen and mysterious underground world existing beneath the rocks. Some of the most challenging and deepest caving routes in Britain, where cavers can enjoy their esoteric pleasures, extend far beneath the surface. But the public can share some of the wonders of the Park's underworld by a visit to the impressive void of Porth yr Ogof in the valley of the Mellte, or the show caverns at the National Showcaves Centre for Wales at Dan yr Ogof in the Tawe Valley.

The best way to see and appreciate the varied and beautiful landscapes which make up the Brecon Beacons National Park is by walking, which is one of the most popular visitor

Sgwd Clun Gwyn – Waterfall Country

Cefn Brynich Bridge, Brecon & Monmouthshire Canal

The historian finds much to enjoy in the Beacons, from the romantic ruins of Carreg Cennen Castle perched on an airy limestone crag near Llandeilo and the concentric towers of Tretower Castle in the Usk Valley near Crickhowell, to the enigmatic Iron Age hillfort of Castell Dinas and the Roman fort of Y Gaer to the west of the county town of Brecon. Llanthony Priory, sheltered in the remote Vale of Ewyas east of the Black Mountains, is the romantic ruin of a monastic retreat dating back to the twelfth century.

There are many traces of early Man in the Brecon Beacons, from hilltop long or round barrows dating from the Neolithic and Bronze Ages, to the 20 or so Iron Age hillforts built and occupied by the Silures – the tribe who also gave their name to one of the oldest rock types found in the area and a geological period now used throughout the world. Next to Castell Dinas, Carn Goch (the red mound) near Llangadog in the Towy Valley is probably the most impressive, covering a vast 30 acres (12ha).

The Romans' regional headquarters of Y Gaer (the fort) is to be found a mile west of the present administrative headquarters of the National Park Authority at Brecon, and formed the hub of a system of Roman roads such as Sarn

Pen y Fan & Corn Du

activities within the National Park. There are routes of varying difficulty to suit everybody, from the challenging ridges of the Beacons to easy, lowland strolling along the 35-mile towpath of the Monmouthshire and Brecon Canal – the only canal which lies almost entirely within a British National Park. Mountain biking is now increasingly popular and there are many routes which can give you a taste of riding the rough stuff. Pony trekking is another very popular outdoor pursuit in the Beacons, and there are many riding schools, especially in the Usk Valley in the north, where horses may be hired to suit all levels of ability.

Brecon Castle and the River Usk

Mountain Centre, Libanus

Helen, which can still be traced by the walker crossing the bleak moorland expanses of Fforest Fawr.

The Park is exceptionally well served by public transport, including the popular Beacons Bus, so you can have the rare pleasure of leaving the car behind to explore these fascinating and ever-changing landscapes. The National Park Visitor Centre (Mountain Centre), with wonderful views of the Beacons on the moorland slopes of Mynydd Illtyd near Libanus, provides a stimulating introduction to the Park and its varied natural and man made features, and makes a great starting point for any exploration.

Sgwd Clun-Gwyn

2. Waterfall Country & The Tawe Valley

Where the rivers Mellte, Hepste, Tawe, Fechan and Pyrddin meet the resistant and impermeable Millstone Grit rocks, they plunge over them, slowly eroding the softer shales and mudstones beneath to create the Beacons' famous Waterfall Country, which is centred on the heavily wooded Mellte and Hepste Valleys near the village of Ystradfellte.

The valley of the Mellte contains a truly delightful series of falls which can be accessed by the visitor on a wonderful walk through Forestry Commission woodland, the names of which all convey the vivid, descriptive poetry of the Welsh language. The Upper Fall, or Sgwd Clun-Gwyn, means "waterfall of the white meadow"; Sgwd Isaf Clun-Gwyn, likened by some to a miniature Niagara, is the "lower white meadow fall", while Sgwd y Pannwr is the "waterfall of the fuller or cloth washer".

Steep-sided gorges abound here, carved out by rushing water, especially in times of flood, as would have happened towards the end of the Ice Ages when huge volumes of sediment-laden meltwater sought a way to the sea far to the south. The cool and shady environment created by these narrow valleys and the trees within them shelter some of the simplest and most ancient groups of plants on Earth. Rare ferns grow from every crack or split in the rocky sides, mosses cover almost every piece of exposed rock and tree, while lichens and liverworts take hold wherever they can.

Some are very fragile and grow very slowly. Mosses specifically help to store moisture, allowing other rarer moisture-loving plants to grow alongside them, but they have weak root systems, making them very easy to dislodge by people clambering in and around the gorges. Some areas have been scraped clean, affecting the humidity of the local environment, potentially causing other species to be lost. All visitors are asked to take special care and keep to defined paths and routes.

Sgwd yr Eira, which translates as "the fall of snow", in the valley of the Hepste, once allowed the careful explorer to get behind its spray-filled curtain, but the natural processes that helped create it now make the overhanging rocks unstable. The waterfall lies within a Special Area of Conservation (SAC) – a European designation providing special protection to a variety of animals, plants and habitats as part of vital global efforts to conserve the world's biodiversity – and for these two reasons access to the waterfall is restricted from time to time to allow any problems to be dealt with (either naturally or through man's intervention) and make it safe again.

From the nearby village of Pontneddfechan, where the Mellte meets the Nedd Fechan, a footpath leads to the 30-foot high Sgwd Gwladus (Lady's fall), on the River Pyrddin. Gwladus, the lady in question, was the specially favoured one of an astonishing 26 daughters of Brychan, a fifth century King of Brycheiniog.

Porth yr Ogof

Further west along the Pyrddin is Sgwd Einion Gam, or "the crooked fall", which abruptly changes direction as it plunges 70 feet through a deep ravine. Perhaps the most easily accessible of the southern waterfalls is the spectacular 90-foot Henrhyd Fall – the highest in South Wales – in the valley of Nant Llech and now in the care of the National Trust.

The natural centres for the exploration of the Park's Waterfall Country are Gwaun Hepste or Cwm Porth car parks near the pretty village of Ystradfellte and the bustling village of Pontneddfechan. From the latter, the industrial past of the area emerges all around, and there is a pleasant walk to the east along the valleys of the Mellte and Sychryd which will take you to the abandoned gunpowder works and silica mines. Part of the train route which linked the mines to the Vale of Neath Canal passes under the towering 150-foot-high crag of Craig y Ddinas, which lies on a major geological fault.

Limestone is a singular rock because it simultaneously creates two quite distinct types of landscape – one above and another below the ground. The Brecon Beacons National Park has a nationally-important area of this strange, topsy-turvy world in the narrow belt of Carboniferous Limestone which runs along the southern edges of the Black Mountains, Fforest Fawr and the Central Beacons.

Formed in part from the remains of countless dead sea creatures beneath the shallow waters of a tropical sea some 350 million years ago, when Britain and the Beacons were on the Equator, the Carboniferous Limestone exhibits all the strange properties that this rock shows wherever it is found throughout the world. The innumerable fissures and joints which criss-cross this rock allow water to run through it. The slight amounts of acid in rain water make this very hard rock slightly soluble, which over thousands of years causes the cracks and fissures to widen leading to the development of entire cave systems. The otherworldly landscape of stalactite and stalagmite decorated caves beneath the hills now delight both tourists and experienced cavers at places like Porth yr Ogof and Dan yr Ogof.

The yawning mouth of Porth yr Ogof, which literally means "gateway to the cave", swallows the River Mellte and is the largest cave entrance in Wales. The cave can be readily accessed from Cwm Porth car park. It has fascinated writers and artists over many centuries, and was once known as White Horse Cave, after the appearance of a series of veins of white calcite on the black wall of rock across the underground lake, just inside the cave entrance, which resemble the head of a horse.

Craig-y-nos Country Park

The impressive, 50-foot wide, 16 foot high entrance the visitor sees is only one of about 14 access points known to the cavers who will often be seen in their bright orange overalls, helmets, ropes and boots, entering this awesome portal. Of course, they delight in exploring the two-mile cave system, but lives have been claimed here too by the swiftly rising water levels caused by heavy rainfall rushing down from the surrounding hilltops to swell the streams and rivers in the valley bottom. Cavers pay great heed to local weather forecasts and conduct a long list of safety checks before entering this dark and challenging world.

A much safer, and probably more enjoyable, way of exploring part of this underground world is to visit Dan yr Ogof, the National Showcaves Centre for Wales, recently voted Britain's Finest Natural Wonder, north of Craig-y-Nos in the Tawe Valley (see box). Above ground a Dinosaur Park and other attractions will fascinate younger visitors, but it's the wonders underground which are the highlight for most. Visitors have dry, safe access to three separate cave systems including the impressive Dome of St Paul's or Cathedral Cave – a vast, echoing chamber which soars for 42 feet (13m) into the solid limestone above your head. Other well-lit formations include the Bone Cave with its fascinating archaeological finds, the Dagger, the Parrot, the Elephant and the Frozen Waterfall.

Nearby 40-acre (16ha) Craig-y-nos Country Park, owned and managed by the National Park Authority and recently awarded an Eco-Centre Green Flag, is the only country park within the National Park. Adjacent to and once the centrepiece of this mature country park is Craig-y-Nos Castle, the former home of the famous opera singer Madame Adelina Patti from 1879. It is now a hotel and still contains many reminders of those days of Victorian elegance and style.

BRITAIN'S FINEST NATURAL WONDER

Don't be surprised if you encounter a tyrannosaurus rex, a triceratops or a stegosaurus on your way into the award-winning Dan yr Ogof National Showcaves Centre for Wales, north of Craig-y-Nos in the Tawe Valley. Recently voted Britain's Finest Natural Wonder, Dan yr Ogof is now also the home of Britain's biggest dinosaur park, houses replica stone circles, an Iron Age village, Shire Horse Centre, Mr Morgan's Farm, Barney Owl's adventure playgound, and a fascinating museum telling the story of limestone. A great rainy day destination.

Dan yr Ogof © GEOPICTURES.NET

Hay Bluff near Hay-on-Wye

3. The Black Mountains

In case you had any doubt that the Black Mountains were Border Country, a glance at the Ordnance Survey map will soon confirm it. In addition to the thousand-year-old earthwork still forming the international boundary between England and Wales and built by King Offa of Mercia during the eighth century, there are castles at Hay-on-Wye, Cusop, Oldcastle, Tretower and Abergavenny (where there was also a Roman fort), and many hill forts and earthworks crown the hilltops.

A walk along the section of Offa's Dyke National Trail as it crosses the lofty Hatterrall Ridge north from Pandy over Hatterrall Hill and Red Darren towards Hay Bluff offers superb views. With the contrasting frowning heights of the parallel ridges of the Black Mountains proper across the Vale of Ewyas to the west, the settled, green, patchwork-quilt landscape of Herefordshire and the Golden Valley stretching away to the east across "the Cat's Back" (Crib y Garth), one feels this really is the end of England and the start of Wild Wales.

It is also the longest and toughest day – 17½ miles (28km) – on the 177-mile Trail which often sorts out 'the men from the boys' and surprises those who were not expecting to have to do some real hill walking. The Trail reaches its highest point on the Red Darren ridge at 2,306ft/703m, before reaching the spectacular viewpoint of Hay Bluff (Pen y Beacon – 2,219ft/ 677m) overlooking the town and the winding valley of the Wye, with the dark, heather-clad hills of Radnorshire beyond.

For the reasons described previously, many of the historic landmarks in the Black Mountains are of a defensive nature, for example the fine hillforts of Castell Dinas and Crug Hywel dating from the Iron Age above the town of Crickhowell in the north, and the castles built by the Norman Marcher lords to protect their lands and boundaries.

Perhaps the most striking of these is Tretower Castle and Court, near Crickhowell, which is an odd example of a castle within a castle, with a twelfth century shell keep entirely enclosed by the nine feet thick walls of Picard's later thirteenth century cylindrical tower. Tretower really gives a history lesson in the defensive architecture of the

Offa's Dyke, Hatterall Ridge

Abergavenny Castle grounds

The other main centre for the exploration of the Black Mountains area, Hay-on-Wye, lies on the extreme northern tip of the National Park. Hay is an ancient market town founded on a bend in the River Wye and watched over by the heavily-restored building known as Hay Castle. But today Hay is best known as the Town of Books (see box), and there are said to be over a million second-hand volumes for sale on its streets.

To the west of the Black Mountains is Talgarth, a small and ancient market town beneath these softly rounded hills, which is an excellent gateway to them for hill walkers or riders. The fourteenth century Pele Tower in the town square is now the Tourist Information Centre. Nearby is Trefeca, the religious settlement which Hywel Harris, the founder of Welsh Methodism, set up in the eighteenth century after experiencing his nonconformist vision in the parish church of St Gwendoline at Talgarth.

To the south of the range is Crickhowell, a thriving and picturesque market town in the Usk Valley, which also provides excellent access to many walking routes in the Black Mountains, with the added appeal of a range of good restuarants and pubs.

Borders, because it stands on the site of an eleventh century motte, and nearby just to the north stands Tretower Court, built in the fourteenth century as a fortified manor house when the threat of invasion had lessened.

The chief town for the exploration of the Black Mountains is the bustling market town of Abergavenny (Y Fenni), which is dominated by the distinctive, isolated hills known as Blorenge, Sugar Loaf and Ysgyryd Fawr. The ruins of Abergavenny Castle stand on a spur of land overlooking the confluence of the Rivers Usk and Gwenny to the south of the town. Traces of the curtain wall and the four-square Great Tower, where the Norman overlord William de Braose treacherously murdered a group of Welsh lords after inviting them to share his Christmas dinner in 1175, still survive and are in the care of Cadw. Abergavenny Castle was probably built on the site of the first century Roman fort of *Gobannivm*. The fourteenth century parish church of St Mary's was likewise built on the site of a Benedictine priory founded by Hamelin de Balun, and there are memorials to the Braose family who originally resided in the priory. Abergavenny Museum is housed in the hunting lodge within the castle grounds and tells the story of this historic market town from prehistory through to the present day.

Further west, the village of Llangynidr has both the Brecon and Monmouthshire Canal and the River Usk running through it. The five locks on the canal to the west of the village lift the canal 50ft (15.2m) in three-quarters of a mile (1.2km) around the slopes of Tor y Foel, and form an attractive feature. The River Usk runs on a rocky bed through rapids here, and is renowned for its excellent trout and salmon fishing. The narrow, single lane Llangynidr Bridge, an ancient monument, leads into the village from the A40 to the north. Nearby attractions include the conifer-fringed Talybont Reservoir and the fascinating Tretower Court and Castle historic house.

The pointed arcade of Early English-style arches framing the Black Mountains beyond is the lasting image of the romantic

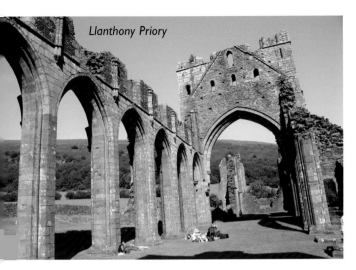

Llanthony Priory

ruin of the original twelfth century priory of Llanthony, in the Vale of Ewyas. The priory was rebuilt under the orders of Hugh de Lacy in 1175. Although the priory, now in the care of Cadw, incorporates the Abbey Hotel in its ruins, it remains the haven of peace and tranquillity which attracted the poet Walter Savage Landor to buy it in 1807. The thirteenth century church dedicated to St David remains.

Reed-fringed Llangors Lake (Llyn Syfaddan), the largest natural lake in South Wales, lies between the Black Mountains and Brecon and supports a wide range of wildlife in its extensive reed beds, swamps and marshy grasslands. This includes birds like great crested grebe, pochard and goosander, while the reeds are home to sedge and reed warblers, reed buntings, and large flocks (the collective name is a 'murmuration') of roosting starlings. The seldom-seen otter, white-clawed crayfish and the medicinal leech, not found anywhere else in the National Park, frequent the quieter reaches of Llangors Lake.

But it also attracts water sport enthusiasts, including power boaters, who once threatened the fragile eco-system which made the lake one of the Park's many Sites of Special Scientific Interest (SSSIs). Now there is a voluntary agreement between the power boaters and the National Park Authority, restricting their use of the one and a half mile long lake to help ensure its tranquillity.

TOWN OF BOOKS

Hay-on-Wye is a booklovers' paradise. Every other shop seems to have racks of second-hand books both in and outside, and the 30 plus bookshops in this bustling little market town even include the former cinema, which has been taken over to become a massive, two-storey emporium of books. This unique bibliographical speciality was started by local entrepreneur Richard Booth of Hay Castle, who at one time also declared independence for Hay from the rest of the UK. A spin-off for the self-styled Town of Books has been the annual Hay Festival of Literature every spring, when top authors from all over the world descend on Hay to give readings and take part in lively discussion panels.

Hay Castle, Hay-on-Wye

Lone walker in the Central Beacons

4. The Central Beacons

The bright russet-red and green striated northern face of Pen y Fan – at 2,907ft/886m the highest point in the Brecon Beacons National Park and also in southern Britain – is one of the finest and most instantly recognisable mountain prospects in the country.

The flat-topped summit, flanked by its almost equally lofty neighbours Corn Du and Cribyn, now all in the care of the National Trust, looks like nothing so much as a neatly-sliced layer-cake, consisting of alternate rust-coloured bands of Old Red Sandstone and green, vegetated Brownstones. Winter snows can seem to add a sprinkling of icing sugar to the whole tempting confection. The range is a constant, imposing barrier to the south as the motorist travels along the A40 through the green valley of the River Usk between Abergavenny and Brecon.

The Central Beacons, with their great scalloped cwms sculpted by Ice Age glaciers – such as Cwm Llwch, Cwm Sere, Cwm Cynwyn and Cwm Oergwm – have been compared to a great breaking wave of sandstones about to crash down and flood the charming Georgian town of Brecon (Aberhonddu) and the valley of the Usk far below.

Brecon is a pleasant county town, founded on the past but looking to the future. The past is represented by the ruins of Bernard de Neufmarche's Norman castle overlooking the confluence of the Usk and the Honddu, and the nearby cathedral church of St Mary Bulwark, which started life as a twelfth century Benedictine priory. Brecon is also blessed with two fine institutions in the Brecknock Museum, in the old assize courts, and the South Wales Borderers' Museum, which includes memories of the important part the regiment played in the defence of Rourke's Drift during the Zulu Wars.

Brecon stands at the northern terminus of the 35-mile Monmouthshire and Brecon Canal, built on a natural shelf above the River Usk between 1799 and 1812 to connect Brecon with the Bristol Channel at Newport. But now it transports holidaymakers rather than coal, iron and limestone in the narrow boats which ply along its sylvan lengths.

Pen y Fan

Pen y Fan from Cribyn

Theatre Brycheiniog, Brecon
© THEATRE BRYCHEINIOG

attempt by invaders to tame the Welsh. But perhaps Crickhowell's greatest glory is its medieval bridge, originally built not long after the castle, which has linked the town with Llangattock (Llangatwg) across the Usk for 800 years, and is still in use by the A4077.

Even today, the Army has a large camp at Sennybridge (Pontsenni) where, in the shadow of forestry-headed Yr Allt, commandos are still being trained in the rigours of mountain warfare on the heights of the Beacons. Soldiers from Sennybridge assisted in the fruitless search for little Tommy Jones (see box), lost on the Beacons in 1900, and they are still often called out to assist in mountain rescue searches for those who underestimate the beckoning Beacons.

The modern but sympathetic red-brick Theatre Brycheiniog stands beside the canal terminus in the centre of the town, and has become the cultural headquarters of the area, with a full programme of events, plays and concerts.

The enclosing wall of the Beacons must have been a constant backdrop to the 500 Roman legionaries and cavalry troops who manned the fort of Y Gaer, now in peaceful farmland about a mile west of Brecon at the confluence of the Rivers Usk and Yscir. This was the regional headquarters for the Roman army as they sought to subdue the unruly Silures who had built the hillforts of Pen y Crug and Slwch Tump on either side of the present town.

The presence of an occupying army seems to be a constant during the long human history of the Central Beacons. Hillforts seem to stud every hilltop and some of the names of their builders are even remembered today in the name of the neighbouring towns. A good example is Crug Hywel – "Howell's Fort" – (also known as Table Mountain) on a spur of Pen Cerrig-calch above the bustling little town of Crickhowell. There's also a ruined thirteenth-century Norman motte and bailey castle here, similar in style to those at Brecon and Abergavenny, showing yet another

The coming of the Neath-Brecon railway in the late 1860's transformed Sennybridge from a sleepy village which hadn't even existed before 1820 to become the bustling market town and the centre of the local community that it is today. Probably best-known for its Army camp, the military history of the Sennybridge area goes back much further, at least to

Y Gaer Roman Fort CADW. CROWN COPYRIGHT

Reconstructed Storey Arms path on Pen y Fan

The village of Pontsticill lies under the wall of the Taf Fechan Reservoir, formerly known as the Pontsticill Reservoir. Completed in 1927 as the last in a chain of four built to supply the needs of fast-expanding Merthyr Tydfil, it swallowed up the earlier Pentwyn Reservoir to the north (which retains its name) and now stretches for over two miles and holds 3,400 million gallons of water. It is the home of a thriving sailing club and with its views of the Beacons to the north is justly popular with visitors.

Running along the eastern shore of the Taf Fechan Reservoir, the two foot gauge Brecon Mountain Railway, one of the famed "Great Little Trains of Wales", provides wonderful views of the Central Beacons: Pen y Fan, Corn Du and Cribyn. Opened in 1980, it runs for five miles using lovingly-restored rolling stock from Pant, three miles north of Merthyr to

Corn Du and Storey Arms

the fourteenth century, when Castell Du, just across the Senni, held offenders who had been caught hunting in the strictly preserved royal hunting forest of Fforest Fawr. Sennybridge also has a range of shops, pubs and a village information agency to cater for the visitor.

But the Central Beacons today are largely peaceful and the haunt of the hill walker, pony-trekker, birdwatcher and tourist. Such is the popularity of the most heavily-used footpath to the reigning summit of Pen y Fan (from the Storey Arms Outdoor Education Centre on the A470 Merthyr-Brecon road) that extensive reconstruction and repair work has had to be carried out by the National Trust. The three-mile route is now paved virtually all the way and provides an easy, but not-to-be-underestimated, ascent to the summit and its wonderful views across the Usk Valley to the north.

Tommy Jones obelisk

Dolygaer, at the foot of Cwm Callan at the northern end of the reservoir. It follows part of the route of the former Merthyr-Brecon line, which opened in 1863 and was closed a century later by the infamous Dr Beeching.

Visitors can learn much about where to go and what to do at the National Park's splendid purpose-built Visitor Centre (Mountain Centre) at Libanus, south west of Brecon off the A470. It stands in splendid isolation on a minor road west of the village on Mynydd Illtyd, itself a moorland outlier to the west of the Central Beacons and commanding superb views of them. The common is named after St Illtud, a Celtic missionary said to be every bit as influential as Pembrokeshire's St David, and is littered with standing stones and ancient earthworks. Bedd Illtud, a cairn west of the Visitor Centre, is said to be his grave.

South of Libanus, just west of the A470 but hidden in a secret, ice-scalloped cwm of the vast, unpopulated moorland mass of Fan Fawr and Fan Dringarth, lies the National Nature Reserve of Craig Cerrig-gleisiad. This 156-acre/63ha site is a rare and now heavily-protected example of what the Beacons looked like before intensive grazing by sheep robbed them of much of the original richness of their plant life.

Over 500 rare plants and flowers usually found in arctic or alpine conditions flourish here among the splintered, broken crags and around its dark bogs, pools and streams. And overhead, you might be lucky enough to glimpse the thrilling sight of a stooping peregrine falcon, or witness the smooth, gliding flight of a red kite.

The Central Beacons are in many respects the honey pot of the National Park, and certainly its footpaths are the heaviest used. But they have managed to retain their mountainous majesty and still reward the discerning visitor who is prepared to leave the car behind with a real taste of freedom and a pervading sense of the continuity of the history of this spectacular, lived-in landscape.

LITTLE TOMMY JONES

The story of five-year-old Tommy Jones, lost on the Beacons for a month in 1900, hit the national newspaper headlines – and prompted one paper to offer the then sizable reward of £20 for news of his whereabouts. Tommy and his father had been visiting his grandparents who lived in the isolated farm of Cwm-llwch beneath Pen y Fan when, with night falling, little Tommy became separated and wandered off. A massive search was organised, but Tommy wasn't found until a Brecon couple came across his body high on the Craig Cwm Llwch ridge a month later. A simple, rugged obelisk now marks the spot, a chilling reminder to walkers that these mountains must always be treated with respect.

Black Mountain

5. The Black Mountain (Mynydd Du)

The Black Mountain, otherwise known as Mynydd Du in Welsh, can truly be called the 'Wild West' of the Brecon Beacons National Park. The most well-known part of the Black Mountain is the ridge known as the Carmarthen Fans — more remote and certainly harder to get to than either the Central Beacons or the eastern Black Mountains, it represents the last great wilderness of the Park.

Llyn y Fan Fach

The scree-buttressed summits of comparatively seldom visited mountains such as Bannau Sir Gaer (749m/2,457ft), Fan Foel (781m/2,562ft), Fan Brycheiniog (802m/2,631ft) and Fan Hir (750m/2,460ft) soar above the legend-haunted lakes of Llyn y Fan Fach and Llyn y Fan Fawr (the lakes of the small and big peaks) and the experienced hill walker can enjoy many hours of exhilarating walking away from the crowds encountered on the only slightly higher summits of Pen y Fan or Cribyn. Views extend north over the conifer-shrouded Usk Reservoir to the Radnorshire Hills.

The geology of the area is identical to the Central Beacons — the fast-eroding layer cake of Old Red Sandstone strata interleaved with the 'filling' of the more vegetated Brownstones. And the finishing touches of the great north-facing cwms such as Waun Sychlwch and Cefn Bryn y Fuwch were carved out by the self-same Ice Age glaciers which created the better-known ones of Cwm Llwch, Cwm Sere, Cwm Cynwyn and Cwm Oergwm in the Central Beacons.

South from these escarpment summits lie the great, sheep-cropped wastelands of Moel Gornach, Garreg Lwyd, Foel

The Carmarthen Fans

Fraith and Garreg Las, which slope down to the Carboniferous Limestone, or karst, scenery of shake and swallow holes, caves and pavements of the Park's limestone belt. To the west the lower ground of Cwm Taldrum and the Rivers Sawdde and Clydach slope down in a chequer-board landscape of small fields and farms to the River Towy. Above the village of Bethlehem – whose Post Office is understandably kept very busy at Christmas time – the twin Iron Age hillforts of mighty Carn Goch tell of more troubled times when defence was obviously important to the local communities. The ruins of the spectacular twelfth century crag-top castle of Carreg Cennen (see box) dominates the lovely Cennen Valley near Llandeilo in much the same way.

East of the reigning Black Mountain summits, there is again much evidence of early human activity, from times when these now barren hills were populated and even cultivated by the earliest settlers. The moorland area above the village of Glyntawe, for example, is littered with those Gothic letters used by the Ordnance Survey to indicate antiquities, such as settlement sites, burnt mounds, hut circles and plat-forms and field systems, all probably dating from the Bronze Age when a kinder climate must have made these hills more habitable and hospitable.

The slopes of Cefn Cul on the western side of the Bwlch Bryn-rhudd Valley, which is followed by the modern A4067 Swansea-Sennybridge road, also feature a number of cigar-shaped pillow mounds, which were used in medieval times to farm rabbits, and which are more often associated with Dartmoor National Park in the south west of England.

Hunting of animals was certainly the prime use of the great Fforest Fawr (Great Forest), a protected area which was set aside as the hunting forest of the Norman first Lord of Brecon, Bernard de Neufmarche, some time in the twelfth or thirteenth centuries. Besides hunting for the pleasure of the nobility, the venison and wild boar taken from the forest were important additions to Brecon's castle larder, and the forest game was jealously watched over by foresters who were able to inflict heavy fines and even the maiming or death of people found offending against the strict forest laws. The medieval forest – an area of open country bearing no resemblance to our modern tree-dominated definition of a 'forest' – was also an important source of fuel, timber and crops such as corn.

The Fforest Fawr Geopark, designated by the European Geoparks Network in 2005 and as a global Geopark by UNESCO in 2006, occupies the whole of the western half of the National Park, including the area of the former medieval forest. One of only 32 in Europe, Fforest Fawr is currently the only Geopark in Wales, and involves the National Park Authority and other partners in working together to conserve the geological heritage through integrated and sustainable development.

A European Geopark is defined as a territory which includes a particular geological heritage and a sustainable development strategy supported by a European development programme. It must contain a number of geological sites of particular importance in terms of its scientific quality, rarity, aesthetic appeal or educational value, and its interest may also be archaeological, ecological, historical or cultural. Fforest Fawr certainly qualifies on all these points, and advertises its magnificent mountains, wonderful waterfalls and spectacular caves.

Another important natural resource is the National Nature Reserve of Craig Cerrig-gleisiad, occupying a crag-bound hollow in the flanks of Fan Frynych just off the A470 north of the Storey Arms. In this huge glacier-carved cwm, rare arctic and alpine flowers bloom among the rocks, and buzzards and ravens soar overhead.

The best centres to explore the wild west of the National Park include Llandovery (Llanymddyfri), an ancient market town just outside the National Park boundary at the

Fan Foel

Llandovery

Monument to Llywelyn ap Gruffydd Fychan, Llandovery Castle

junction of the A4069, the A40 and the A483. It is also at the junction of three rivers – the Bran, Gwydderig and Tywi – and was originally founded by the Romans who found Welsh gold at nearby Pumsaint. Llandovery was given its market charter by Richard III and later became an important drovers' town, where herds of cattle up to 30,000 strong, plus pigs and even geese and turkeys were gathered to be driven across country to markets in London.

Further west on the A483 on the River Tywi is another bustling market town, Llandeilo, which was named after the fifth century Saint Teilo, and was a former centre for tanning, corn and woollen mills. On the outskirts of Llandeilo in grounds landscaped by Capability Brown is Dinefwr Castle, ancestral home of the Rhys family, who also built Carreg Cennen Castle (see box) in the twelfth century, and now in the care of the National Trust.

Sennybridge, a small market town, is another good centre from which to explore the Black Mountain. Probably best-known for its Army camp just outside the town, the military history of the Sennybridge area goes back to the fourteenth century, when Castell Du, just across the Senni, held offenders who had been caught hunting in the strictly preserved royal hunting forest of Fforest Fawr.

Trecastle (Trecastell) is an old coaching village named after its early twelfth century motte and bailey castle built by Bernard de Neufmarche – the largest example of its kind in the National Park. North west of the village on the summit of Mynydd Bach Trecastell are the scant remains of the two Roman camps known as Y Pigwn.

Returning to the myth-haunted summits of the Black Mountain, the hamlet of Myddfai is situated at their foot and was the home of the farmer who fell in love with and married the fairy lady of Llyn y Fan Fach (see Chapter 8, Legends, culture and customs for the full story) and later the famous Meddygon Myddfai, or the Physicians of Myddfai.

Carreg Cennen

Carreg Cennen Castle

Carreg Cennen must be one of the most spectacularly-sited castles in Britain. It stands on the edge of a sheer limestone crag rising from woodland 300 metres above the green Cennen Valley and has magnificent views of the Black Mountain. Founded by Lord Rhys of Dinefwr in the twelfth century, it stands on the site of even earlier fortifications. The castle has had a troubled history. In one decade of the thirteenth century, it changed hands about four times, and it was besieged by Owain Glyndwr among others. Don't miss the spooky 200-foot long underground tunnel reached from inside the castle walls, which burrows through the face of the crag.

Dinefwr Castle CADW. CROWN COPYRIGHT

Buzzard © LAURIE CAMPBELL

6. Wildlife of the Beacons

It was a stiff climb up from the picnic site on the A470 just north of the Storey Arms to reach the 2,063ft (629m) summit of Craig Cerrig-gleisiad, a huge hollow bitten out of the flanks of Fan Frynych by the grinding power of an Ice Age glacier.

Our ranger guide assured us that this was one of Wales's top wildlife sites, recognised by the fact that it was a specially-protected National Nature Reserve, one of seven in the Brecon Beacons National Park. But on this misty, autumnal day there didn't seem to be much wildlife to see.

Mists wreathed the weathered crags of the shattered, 550-foot (150m) cliff face below our feet and beneath we could just make out the scree slopes and humps and bumps of the moraines left behind by that massive cwm-cutting glacier over 10,000 years ago. In that cliff face and the boggy land below, we were told, grew over 500 different species of plants, many of them rare arctic-alpine survivors dating back to the cwm's creation during the last Ice Age. These include the spreading, bright crimson stars of purple saxifrage and the fleshy-leaved, golden-flowered roseroot, a member of the stonecrop family.

It is the unique chemistry of the rocks – where the acidic sandstones abut the lime-rich alkaline brownstones of the Old Red Sandstone – which enable this varied range of arctic-alpines to flourish. Plus the fact, of course, that the steep crags do not allow the nibbling teeth of even the most voracious of Welsh mountain sheep to reach them to cut them off in their prime.

The rich flora of these inaccessible crags in turn attracts a wide range of insect life, including dragonflies in nearby boggy mountain pools, and no less than 16 species of butterflies, one of which is the startling emerald-winged green hairstreak. And feeding on these insects are special birds like the white-bibbed ring ouzel – a tuneful mountain blackbird – and perky summer visitors like the wheatear and stonechat.

We were just pondering on this unseen wealth of wildlife when suddenly, the mists cleared away and we could at last appreciate the full majesty of our viewpoint, with the smooth slopes of the Central Beacons sweeping away to their distant summits in the east across Glyn Tarell. Then just as suddenly there was a swoosh of wind and a magnificent bronze-winged buzzard zoomed over our heads to swoop majestically down into the cwm below.

It was one of those treasured moments that you will always remember, and as we descended back down into the valley, accompanied by the sinister croaking of a pair of jet-black ravens, we realised why Craig Cerrig-gleisiad was so important, and so fully deserved its NNR status.

Other National Nature Reserves in the Park include Ogof Ffynnon Ddu, near Penwyllt, some parts of which were

Peregrine falcon © LAURIE CAMPBELL

quarried in the past for limestone. This reserve exhibits all the classic "karst" features of a Carboniferous Limestone landscape, from limestone pavements rich in shy plants such as lily of the valley and hart's tongue fern, to sink or swallow holes and caves. The protected area encompasses the hill-tops of Carreg Cadno and Carreg Lwyd where if you are lucky you may see some of the 39 species of birds found here, including peregrine falcons, wheatears and ravens.

Another limestone NNR is the impressive Craig y Cilau escarpment near Llangattock, part of which was once also quarried for limestone for the ironworks in nearby Nantyglo as well as for local farmers to "sweeten" their pastures. The 400-foot (122m) crag in the north east of the reserve is one of the largest limestone cliffs in south Wales, and from the footpath which runs beneath its slopes, you can see some of the very rare least whitebeam trees still tenaciously clinging on in crevices in the precipitous rock face.

In total contrast, the Coed y Cerrig NNR near Llanvihangel Crucorney, north of Abergavenny, is an ancient deciduous woodland on the lower, eastern slopes of the Black Mountains. Beneath the oak, ash and beech trees grow floral rarities such as the nettle-leaved bellflower and the ghostly white, chlorophyll-free parasite, the toothwort. In the wet valley bottom, occasionally coppiced alders grow over sedges and other wet loving plants. There is a board-walk (which is accessible to all) so visitors' feet stay dry. All three species of British woodpecker – green, greater and lesser spotted – tap away to announce their presence, and tuneful summer migrants include the pied flycatcher, redstart and blackcap.

The beech woodlands of the Cwm Clydach NNR, lying between Gilwern and Brynmawr, represent one of the largest area of native beech in Wales, at the western edge of its natural range in Britain, and are the home of a variety of birds, butterflies and insects. The River Clydach has formed a deep gorge, once utilised for iron-making, but where today yew and whitebeam trees cling precariously to the cliffs. In the shade created by the beeches, ground plants other than mosses, fungi and rarities such as the bird's nest orchid, are relatively sparse. Some of these mosses and fungi are very rare too. A good range of woodland birds can be seen, including all three species of woodpecker, nuthatch, sparrowhawk, kestrel and tawny owl.

The sixth and latest NNR is Cwm Cadlan, an oasis of wildlife on the edge of the National Park, and one of the largest examples of fen meadowland in Wales, studded with rare, lime-loving wildflowers and their associated insects. The NNR lies in the middle of the Nant Cadlan Valley, much of which is also covered by SSSI protection. It includes some of the best globeflower meadows in the Park, and at the other end of the valley, the Blaen Cynon Special Area of Conservation includes a population of one of Europe's most threatened butterflies – the marsh fritillary. The seventh NNR – the Dan yr Ogof Showcaves – are managed as a visitor attraction by the owners, who provide free educational visits for schools.

Another entirely different habitat is provided by water, and although the Park's many reservoirs do not support a vast range of aquatic wildlife, the largest natural lake, Llangors Lake (Llyn Syfaddan), at the foot of the Black Mountains, is much richer. The reed-fringed expanse attracts many birds, from the great crested grebe to ducks like pochard and goosander, while the reeds themselves are home to sedge and reed warblers, reed buntings, and huge flocks of roosting starlings. Also present are the elusive otter, the white-clawed crayfish and the medicinal leech, which is not found anywhere else in the Park. The lake is designated as a Site of Special Scientific Interest (SSSI),

One of the great ornithological conservation success stories of recent years has been the return of the graceful red kite to the skies above the National Park (see box). The national population of red kites had shrunk to a handful of pairs which clung on in mid Wales, but protection programmes and gradual re-introductions elsewhere by the RSPB put the number of breeding pairs up to 50 by the mid-1980s. There are now thought to be at least 500 breeding pairs in Wales, and they have become an almost common sight over the deciduous woodlands of the Beacons.

Another Beacons speciality which walkers, particularly on the Cwm Cynwyn bridleway in the Black Mountains or on Llangors Common, may come across, is the small, shaggy Welsh Mountain ponies. Contrary to common belief, these are not wild at all but are owned by local farmers who run them on the hill all year round. Once popular as children's riding ponies, their real value now lies in the contribution they can make to the conservation of the areas they graze.

The latest area of the Brecon Beacons to receive special protection is the entire western side of the National Park including the Central Beacons, the Black Mountain and

The Crannog, Llangors Lake

The Local Biodiversity Action Plan in action

Fforest Fawr, which was designated a European Geopark in 2005. Fforest Fawr Geopark is currently the only UNESCO-approved global Geopark in Wales, and one of only six in Britain. The idea behind the European Geopark Network is that the 30 or so designated sites should work together to conserve their geological heritage through integrated and sustainable development.

The deciding factor which qualified the area for this rare distinction was the combination of the three marked types of scenery created by the succession of Millstone Grit, Carboniferous Limestone and Old Red Sandstone rocks. The National Park Authority now works with its partners in the network to come up with sustainable policies aimed at protecting and promoting its special geological heritage.

It was the need to protect the incredibly rich diversity of wildlife dependent on the underlying geology which encouraged the National Park Authority, in partnership with seven other local organisations, to create a Park-wide Local Biodiversity Action Plan – titled *Our Natural World* .

Local Biodiversity Action Plans (LBAPs) are the UK Government's method of delivering the commitment to conserve wildlife by signing the UN Convention on Biological Diversity. *Our Natural World* details those habitats and species of principle importance for conserving biodiversity within the National Park and outlines the various action partners such as the National Trust, Wildlife Trusts, Forestry Commission and the National Park Authority will take to ensure wildlife is conserved for the future.

The National Park believes that this approach will emphasise the intrinsic role of landowners, local communities and visitors in managing and utilising the natural environment in a lasting, sustainable way. It sees its own role as assisting local groups and individuals to develop and implement projects and initiatives which will deliver the targets of the Local Biodiversity Action Plan.

FLYING KITES IN THE BEACONS

A welcome returning sight in the skies above the Brecon Beacons, especially in well-wooded areas, is the graceful chestnut red raptor, the red kite. This scavenging bird of prey was a common sight even in cities like London in Tudor times. But due to persecution, egg-stealing and the long-term effects of DDT on their reproduction, the national population came perilously close to extinction. Successful protection programmes instituted by the RSPB, and the setting-up of feeding stations for kites at places like Llanddeusant and Gigrin Farm, near Rhayader in Powys, have seen the population explode, to the extent that mid-Wales is now also known as 'Kite Country.' The distinctive, V-shaped tails of this elegant bird of prey now once again form an exciting addition to the birdwatchers' tick list in the Beacons.

Red kite © LAURIE CAMPBELL

Langors Lake

7. A Beacons Timeline

10,000-5,000 years ago
Mesolithic (Middle Stone) Age

The first hunter-gathers move into the Brecon Beacons following the end of the last Ice Age. Earliest evidence of them is found in the tiny slivers of flint known as microliths, sometimes uncovered in the peat of the hills at upland sites like Waun Fignen Felen and Mynydd Myddfai, which provide the only evidence of the people who first hunted here.

5,000-4,000 years ago
Neolithic (New Stone) Age

The first farmers arrive, living in small, isolated settlements. They leave behind little or no trace of their field systems, so all that remains are their ritual monuments, such as the chambered tombs of Ty-isaf near Talgarth in the Rhiangoll Valley, Gwernvale near Crickhowell and Ty Iltud long cairn at Llanhamlach in the Usk Valley, and burial cairns on the hilltops.

4,000-3,000 years ago
Bronze Age

Burial mounds (or cairns) and isolated standing stones, such as Maen Llia between Ystradfellte and Sennybridge; Maen Llwyd at the head of the Grwyne Fechan Valley in the eastern Black Mountains, and Maen Mawr near the source of the River Tawe on the Black Mountain, are the scant but most obvious features left behind by the mysterious Bronze Age people.

3,000-2,000 years ago
Iron Age

The age of the hillforts leaves its distinctive mark across the Beacons landscape, with at least 50 known examples, the most impressive of which are at Carn Goch near Llangadog in the Black Mountain, at 30 acres/12ha one of the largest in Wales, and Castell Dinas and Crug Hywel near Crickhowell. Hut circles inside some of these suggest that a few of these forts, probably constructed by the warlike Silures tribe, were permanent settlements while others were used as summer dwellings or even market places.

Maen Llia

Carn Goch hillfort and the Towy Valley

Sarn Helen Roman Road

2,000-1,000 years ago
Age of the Saints

Christianity spreads slowly into the hills and valleys of the Beacons, inspired by influential figures like St David and St Illtud, but the Age of the Saints in the Beacons are dominated by Offa, King of Mercia. He constructs the still-formidable barrier of his Dyke from the Bristol Channel to the Irish Sea as a physical and political separation between his kingdom and the Welsh sometime during the eighth century (see box).

1000 –1200AD
Norman Conquest

The Normans impose their authority on the land by building the first castles of timber, 'motte and bailey', construction at Brecon and Bronllys. These are followed by more substantial stone-built structures of the Marcher (border) lords, such as those at Crickhowell, Llandovery and Tretower. Manor houses and churches, including the religious house, Llanthony Priory, are built in the villages, and the great 40,000-acre hunting forest of Fforest Fawr (the Great Forest of Brecknock) is created for the use of the nobility.

2,000 years ago
Roman Period

The Romans set up their headquarters at Y Gaer, a mile west of Brecon at the confluence of the Rivers Usk and Yscir, which could accommodate 500 cavalry troopers. The legionnaires supervise and adapt the construction of their usually ruler-straight roads to switchback up steep slopes and follow the contours of the hilly landscape across the Beacons. There are great views from the Roman road, Sarn Helen, which linked Y Gaer with Nidum (Neath) across Fforest Fawr, and the route which passes the remains of the two temporary marching camps at Y Pigwn on its way to Llandovery.

Bronllys Castle
CADW. CROWN COPYRIGHT

1200-1400
Middle Ages

Cultivation of the valleys and the use of the hill pastures for common grazing continues into the Middle Ages. Markets are set up in the major villages and towns, and fine churches such as the priory churches at Brecon Cathedral and St Mary's Church at Abergavenny, are built by wealthy landlords. The present stone castle of Carreg Cennen was built as an English outpost by one of Edward I's barons.

Ironworks remains, Clydach Gorge

Carreg Cennen Castle

1400-1700
Tudors and Stuarts

This is the age of the large landowners and the creation of the large country houses, estates and landscaped parklands around the edge of the mountains. Farming remains the dominant local industry, although iron-making starts in the Clydach Gorge between Gilwern and Brynmawr as early as the seventeenth century, and there are other forges constructed on the fast-flowing rivers of the Beacons.

1700 – 1850
Industrial Revolution

The first improved roads and turnpikes in the Beacons date from 1767. The 35-mile Monmouthshire and Brecon Canal is built between 1799 and 1812 to transport coal, lime and wool between Brecon and Newport, but large-scale industrialisation is mostly confined to the valleys to the south of the present National Park, where Blaenavon becomes an important and early centre for iron production.

1850-1900
Victorian Britain

The Railway Age dawns, and the county town of Brecon is soon linked by rail with Merthyr in the south in 1863, Neath in the west (in 1867) and Hay-on-Wye (in 1864) to the east. At the same time, the first tourists start to visit the Beacons, and the area is made popular by visitors such as the famous opera singer Madam Adelina Patti, who comes to live at Craig-y-Nos Castle in 1879.

1900-1970
Modern Britain

Major engineering works create a total of 18 reservoirs, such as Talybont-on-Usk, Pontsticill and Llyn-onn, as the towns and cities of the South Wales valleys realise the water-gathering potential of the area. The Brecon Beacons National Park – the tenth in Britain – is finally designated in 1957. In the 1960s, as the Beeching axe falls on the railways, the fast-expanding population of the industrial valleys increasingly use their cars to reach the Beacons for their recreation, a trend that has continued into the twenty first century.

Monmouthshire & Brecon Canal

OFFA'S DYKE

Offa's Dyke, the 142-mile long embankment and boundary between England and Wales, has stood virtually untouched for over a thousand years, and is best seen in the Park as it winds along the ridge above the Vale of Ewyas. It was built by King Offa of Mercia some time during the eighth century to form a controllable political boundary between his land to the east and the wild Welsh tribes to the west, from sea to sea between the Bristol Channel to the Irish Sea. Today, almost its entire length is followed by the 177-mile Offa's Dyke National Trail, which was opened in 1971.

Above the Vale of Ewyas

Llyn y Fan Fach and the Carmarthen Fans

8. Legends, Culture and Customs

As you might expect for a remote mountain fastness like the Brecon Beacons, myths and legends hang in the remote cwms and valleys like the mists which so often fill them and blanket their summits.

Perhaps the most famous is that of the Lady of the Lake and the Physicians of Myddfai, which is centred on the mysterious lake of Llyn y Fan Fach which lies hidden under the grim precipices of the Carmarthen Fans in the heart of the Black Mountain (Mynydd Du). The story goes that a local farmer from the nearby hamlet of Myddfai took his flock of sheep up to the lake one day and as he sat by the shore eating his lunch, he was surprised by a beautiful woman who emerged from its dark waters.

He offered her some bread, but she refused him until he eventually brought her some unleavened bread, which she at last accepted. They fell in love, and she promised to marry him if her father consented. The next time he went up to the lake, she emerged with her father and her four identical sisters. The father said he could have the lady and as many cattle and sheep as he could count, provided he picked out the right daughter.

She cleverly tipped him off by wriggling her toe when he came to her, and the marriage was agreed on the condition that if he should strike her three times with iron, she would return to the lake, taking her generous dowry with her. Of course, after several years of happy marriage, the inevitable happened; the taboo was accidently broken on three occa-

sions and the fairy woman returned to the lake taking the sheep and cattle with her.

But that is not the end of the story, because the couple had five sons on whom their fairy mother imparted the mystic secrets of healing, and the sons became the most famous physicians in Wales – known as the Physicians of Myddfai. This line of doctors and herbal healers lasted for over six centuries, and the last known Physician of Myddfai, Dr C Rice Williams, died in 1842 at Aberystwyth.

It is easy to dismiss this tale of fairies and lake-dwellers in today's cynical age, but some scholars have linked the tale with the transition from the culture of the Bronze Age to that of the Iron Age, and the suspicions local people might have had with the revolutionary new metal. The Lady of the Lake is claimed to be a member of the *Tylwyth Teg*, or the Fairy Folk who inhabit these remote places in the hills, and could well have represented the older, pre-Christian Celtic order.

There's no record of the Myddfai farmer offering his fairy bride a love spoon, but the chances are that he might well have. The Brecknock Museum in Brecon has one of the finest displays of these intricately-carved love spoons (*llwy caru* in Welsh), which were a kind of wooden love token or engagement ring signifying the betrothal of a couple. If the spoon was returned, the lady wasn't interested.

The Welsh language plays an integral and increasingly-important part in the cultural life of the National Park, and visitors

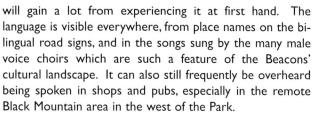
Bi-lingual road signs

Aberhonddu & District Male Choir ©THE CHOIR

will gain a lot from experiencing it at first hand. The language is visible everywhere, from place names on the bilingual road signs, and in the songs sung by the many male voice choirs which are such a feature of the Beacons' cultural landscape. It can also still frequently be overheard being spoken in shops and pubs, especially in the remote Black Mountain area in the west of the Park.

Don't be afraid to ask local people if you are unsure how a local name is pronounced. Some sounds spoken in Welsh are very different from their English equivalents, and can be quite difficult for English-speaking tongues to master. As a rough guide, that awkward double 'l' sound, as in Llandeusant, Llandovery or Llandeilo, is pronounced by placing the tongue on the upper roof of the mouth near the upper teeth, as if ready to pronounce an "l", then blowing, rather than voicing, the "l". Try it – it's not too difficult and once you've mastered it, you'll never forget.

Commonly-heard greetings include *bore da* – good morning; *nos da* – good night; *hwyl* – cheers; *croeso* – welcome, and *lechyd da* – good health. Place names are usually very descriptive in Welsh, as the table of common names in the box shows. Religious nonconformism has always been very strong in the Welsh hills, and the Beacons became a cockpit of this move-

ment against the teachings of the established church. One of the earliest nonconformist preachers was Hywel Harris of Trefeca near Talgarth, an interesting man who was also an innovative farmer and founder of the Brecknockshire Agricultural Society – one of the first in the country – in 1755. Harris also set up an early commune of agricultural workers known as "The Family" or "Connexion" at Trefeca – a kind of forerunner of the hippy communes of the 1960s.

One of the many people influenced by the far-sighted Harris was William Williams Pantycelyn, of Pantycelyn, near Llandovery (as was common, he took his name from his home) on the western side of the Park. Williams was one of the leading figures in the Methodist Revival which swept across Wales in the eighteenth century, and he was also one of our greatest hymn writers – responsible for, among others, the stirring *Guide me, O Thou Great Jehovah*. Shortly before he died in 1791, Williams estimated that he had travelled nearly 150,000 miles in his long lifetime of preaching the Gospel to the people of Wales.

The Beacons seem always to have attracted artists and rebels, among whom was Eric Gill, the famous artist, sculptor and designer of typefaces, who came to live at Capel-y-ffin, the former monastery of Father Ignatius, in the shadow of the Black Mountains, in the 1920s. Gill's free-spirited and free-loving Bohemian existence must have caused some raised eyebrows among his strictly nonconformist neighbours. Just across the valley is The Vision farmstead, where the award-winning author Bruce Chatwin set his best-selling book *On the Black Hill*, which explores the close relationship between two bachelor farmer brothers.

Another artist who made the Beacons her home was the internationally-famed opera singer Madame Adelina Patti, who set up home at Craig-y-Nos Castle in the valley of the Upper Tawe in 1879. Tales of the concerts that she gave in the small, purpose-built theatre in the Gothic Revival castle are legendary and they attracted many of the leading figures of the day, including members of the royal family. Ironically, her favourite song was said to be the rather prosaic "Home Sweet Home." Madame Patti was enormously rich – she was said to be able to command £1,000 for a performance – which gave her the wealth to refurbish the Gothic fantasy of a castle in the depths of the Welsh hills. The castle, now a hotel, was once the centrepiece to the adjacent 40-acre (16ha) Craig-y-nos Country Park, the only country park within the National Park, and recently awarded an Eco-Centre Green Flag.

It just wouldn't be Wales without singing, and many towns and villages have their own Male Voice Choirs, many of which welcome audiences. Bringing the culture of the Beacons bang up to date, every summer the eyes and ears of the jazz world turn to the unlikely venue of Brecon for the Brecon Jazz Festival, as the sleepy market town becomes the Welsh equivalent of New Orleans. Founded nearly 25 years ago by the veteran jazzman and local resident George Melly, the festival attracts many major international names and emerging talents, and over 17,000 jazz lovers throng the streets to attend a total of 80 concerts on various stages and venues throughout the town.

And of course the Hay-on-Wye Literature Festival, held appropriately enough in the second-hand book capital of Britain, is an annual treat for booklovers and attracts some of the top authors for readings and lectures every year.

Craig-y-nos Castle © CRAIG-Y-NOS

UNDERSTANDING PLACENAMES

A table of common placenames used in Welsh, with their English equivalents:-

- ❖ Aber: river mouth
- ❖ Afon: river
- ❖ Allt: hill, slope, wood
- ❖ Bach or fach: small
- ❖ Ban (plural bannau): peak, crest
- ❖ Castell: castle
- ❖ Coed: wood
- ❖ Du or ddu: black
- ❖ Dwr: water
- ❖ Eglwys: church
- ❖ Eira: snow
- ❖ Fawr or mawr: great or big
- ❖ Ffordd: way, road
- ❖ Hen: old
- ❖ Heol: road
- ❖ Isaf: lower, lowest
- ❖ Llan or eglwys: church
- ❖ Llyn: lake
- ❖ Mynydd: mountain
- ❖ Nos: night
- ❖ Ogof: cave
- ❖ Pen: top
- ❖ Sgwd or rhaeadr: waterfall
- ❖ Ty: house
- ❖ Uchaf: upper, highest
- ❖ Ystrad: valley floor

Fresh local produce from the National Park

smallfarms
organically produced food

Farm Shop
and N
ww

9. A Taste of the Beacons

The chances are that at some time you will have ordered and enjoyed a full English breakfast in your hotel or bed and breakfast holiday accommodation. But why not try a full *Welsh* breakfast (*brecwast Cymreig llawn*) while you are staying in the Brecon Beacons National Park?

According to a recipe by Lee Evans of The Manor, Crickhowell, in the recently-published *Black Mountains Breakfast Book*, this local delicacy consists of locally-produced bacon, sausages, laverbread, tomatoes, oatmeal, eggs and sliced mushrooms. Rashers of the bacon are wrapped around the sausages, and then cakes consisting of laverbread, oats and chopped bacon are made up into burgers with a filling of tomatoes, all topped with a poached egg.

There's nothing else quite like it, and there's no doubt that a Black Mountains breakfast would make a great start to any day. It should certainly keep you going without the need for further nourishment for a few hours as you ascend Ysgyryd Fawr, the National Trust's Sugar Loaf, or take a stroll along the roller-coaster Offa's Dyke National Trail.

Among several other more exotic recipes in this excellent little booklet, produced as the result of a 'breakfast challenge' by the National Park Authority in partnership with adventa, Medrwm and the Mid Wales Tourism Partnership, is laverbread souffles. Laverbread, for readers who are unsure, is a local Welsh and West Country delicacy consisting of thin, reddish-purple and green fronds of edible seaweed, and although the Black Mountains may be a long way from the sea, the souffle is certainly mouth-watering.

Laverbread is also used with the local specialist cheese Y Fenni (the Welsh name for Abergavenny) to create laverbread rissoles and laverbread bread plaits. Other recipes include vegetarian options such as Glamorgan sausages combined with apples to create a delicious compote; while Welsh Penderyn whisky can be flamed to produce a caramelised breakfast porridge.

Full Welsh breakfast

Images from Brecon Beacons and Hay Food Festivals

According to Nerys Howell, a celebrity food consultant who has waved the flag for Welsh food and drink across the world, the food scene in Wales and the Brecon Beacons is thriving. "Food and drink is an essential part of the experience of a visit to this area," says Nerys, "and these recipes reflect the flavours which are unique to this region."

From the growing numbers of local food festivals and farmers' markets, to the many small producers and award-winning restaurants and hotels, local food has become a subject on everyone's lips – but not for too long!

Perhaps the best places to really appreciate the Beacons spectacular range of locally-produced foods are at those local food festivals, which are held throughout the year. The Hay-on-Wye Food Festival takes place in June, Abergavenny's in September, and Brecon's in October. These are the occasions when food producers, celebrity chefs, local communities and visitors all come together to celebrate the richness of the food culture of the Brecon Beacons. It's no exaggeration to say that these festivals are a gourmet's delight.

The two ever-popular farmers' markets in the Park, where you can meet and chat with the producers themselves, are held at Abergavenny on the fourth Thursday of every month, and at Brecon on the second Saturday of each month. Here you can talk to the farmer who produced that delicious rack of Welsh lamb you enjoyed the evening before, or ask the dairyman what goes into that scrumptious local cheese or ice cream.

The number of good places to eat in the National Park is growing fast, whatever the size of your budget might be. Many gourmet awards have been won by Beacons hotels, pubs and restaurants, and it is well worth looking out for them. And more and more locally-produced and organic food is finding its way into the kitchens of hotels and bed and breakfast providers, pubs and restaurants, giving you the opportunity to experience the very best of the local flavours. And if it's not obvious, make sure you ask if there is locally produced food on the menu.

What could be better after a day's hiking on the Beacons than enjoying a meal of lamb raised up on the mountains you have just walked across, with vegetables from the small-holding down the road and cheese from the local dairy? All this is usually put together by chefs who understand the character of the place and can put a real local emphasis into the delicious flavours.

Brecknock Farmers' Market, Brecon Market Hall

Brecon Beacons Food Festival, Brecon

PENCAE MAWR FARM FOODS

Handmade Organic Vegetarian Produce

And while on your walking tour, you could always stop at a local pub or inn for lunch, making sure you look out for local produce on the menu. Then complete your day by allowing your taste buds to enjoy a real Welsh treat by relaxing in a restaurant or hotel and selecting for your main course either some Welsh Black beef, Welsh venison or Welsh lamb cutlets. For dessert, try a local cheese like Y Fenni, Welsh heather honey, and delicious local ice cream, just to name a few. And you could always finish off with a liqueur consisting of Penderyn whisky.

And wherever you stay or eat in the Brecon Beacons National Park, make sure you look out for the Green Dragon symbol. This means that your accommodation or food provider – whether it be a top hotel or a modest village bed and breakfast – has passed the strict criteria to become a part of this unique environmental accreditation scheme. The Green Dragon scheme works by supporting businesses who show practical improvements in things like energy consumption and efficiency, recycling, transport and the careful use of water.

The Green Dragon scheme was set up by the National Assembly for Wales and is now managed by Arena Network for the National Park. The publicity for the scheme states: "It gives you the confidence that your hosts are looking after the environment every bit as carefully as they look after you."

The Beacons have become the home of many working craftspeople since the days when local farmers carved love spoons for their intended brides (see box). Today these craftspeople range from the talented artists and painters who exhibit in the many local galleries found in the towns and villages, to the hand-forged ironwork produced at the forges at Bronllys and Llanellen, and glassworks like that at the Gate Gallery in Brecon town centre. There really is something to suit all tastes – and pockets – as you explore the craft shopping opportunities of the Beacons.

A STIRRING GIFT OF LOVE

The Brecknock Museum in Brecon has one of the finest displays of intricately-carved love spoons (*llwy caru* in Welsh), which were carved mainly between the seventeenth and nineteenth centuries by would-be suitors during the long winter nights in many Welsh-speaking Beacons farmsteads, but they represent a tradition which probably goes back even further. They come in all shapes and sizes, but all are traditionally carved from one piece of wood. From this was fashioned a spoon or spoons which were decorated with extraordinarily elaborate motifs such as inter-locking chains, hearts, bells, foliage, padlocks and keys. Some love spoons had slotted hollow round or rectangular handles, inside which little wooden balls were somehow carved. The number of these balls supposedly represented the number of children the couple hoped to have after their marriage.

Abergavenny Food Festival

10. Taking a Break from the Car

Unless you have actually done it, it's hard to explain the sense of freedom you can feel simply by leaving the car at home. Suddenly, you don't have to worry about the stress and strain of driving and negotiating traffic, the need to navigate your way to your destination without getting lost, and the nagging worry of finding somewhere to park.

You can enjoy the countryside far better too from the comfortable seat of a bus or train, without having to be constantly looking where you are going. You'll be surprised at what you've missed sitting behind the wheel of a car. Suddenly you can see over walls and hedgerows as the countryside with all its glorious views is opened up to you.

Of course, most of the visitors to the Brecon Beacons National Park still arrive by car simply because it's more convenient. But even if you have got here by car, try leaving it at your accommodation for a day – or even a week. Why bother with the stress of driving when you are on holiday – leave that for when you have to get back to work.

All sorts of fascinating places can be reached without having to get in the car. If you are reasonably fit and active, you can probably walk to many of them from where you are staying anyway. And of course if you have brought your bikes, you will have an even wider range of choices. You can also hire bikes here – many places will deliver to your accommodation. Ask your host or visit www.cyclebreconbeacons.com

Just look out for accommodation and attractions with the bus symbol. Then ask for the free *Discover the Beacons* guide for loads of ideas of things to do and places to go without the car. There is full timetable information available in a separate Travel Guide available via the website or from Information Centres.

And if walking is your passion, remember that you can see far more if you don't have to walk back to the beginning – head over the hills or amble along the canal and then get the bus back. There will be no problems about stopping for a drink en route either.

The Beacons Bus is also there to take you into and around the National Park on summer Sundays and Bank Holidays.

Mountain biking on the Gap Road above Cwm Cynwyn

The service is specially designed for visitors and takes you to many of the area's best known villages and attractions. The Cardiff Brecon Bike Bus service even tows a bike trailer to Brecon and then runs between there and Abergavenny all day long. Other buses will take you up into the mountains, to the National Park's Visitor Centre at Libanus; the Gardens of Carmarthenshire; the Brecon Mountain Railway; Hay-on-Wye, Llangors Lake and much more besides.

But even better, you can use the Beacons Bus to take you walking. There is a booklet of linear walks you can do using the bus available from Information Centres and from the website. For example, if you are starting from any of the cities and towns of South Wales, such as Swansea, Porthcawl, Bridgend, Cardiff or Newport, the Beacons Bus will take you to the heart of the National Park at Brecon stopping at most of the villages and attractions en route and enabling you to do linear walks between stops. Or if you are staying in Brecon, you can catch the Beacons Bus Roundabout service and it will take you out and about throughout the Park all day, returning you safe and sound back at Brecon in the late afternoon after an excellent day out, without the worry of traffic and parking.

Walkers in the Central Beacons

Beacons Bus, Brecon

The Offa's Dyke Flyer is another part of Beacons Bus service and takes you from Hay-on-Wye up to Hay Bluff, to Llanthony Priory and all the fascinating villages in the valley. This fabulous circuit then returns to the east of the mountains, enabling you to do some fantastic linear walks along the Offa's Dyke National Trail, such as the airy and strenuous Hatterall Ridge.

The Beacons Bus will bring you back to the start of your walk or cycle ride, and if you'd like to get off at an attraction and catch the next bus home, you can always do so. Pick up a timetable leaflet locally to find out more. Half the fun can often be the planning of your route and the services you'll use, plus where you'd like to visit, in advance.

Jazz on the Heart of Wales line: September to May each year.
© HEART OF WALES LINE

travellers can get to Brecon via Cardiff and to Abergavenny via Birmingham. In addition, the TrawsCambria network has a regular two-hour service from Cardiff and Newtown/Llandrindod Wells.

Brecon Beacons National Park is very convenient from London and the south east of England, and it is well served by the motorway network of the M4, M5 and M50. In fact, it is easily accessible by road from all parts of the UK.

If you are coming by car from southern England, most people go via the M4 to Newport and Abergavenny on the A4042. If coming from the Midlands or northern England the most direct route is via the M5 taking the Ross Spur (M50) to Ross-on-Wye and then to Abergavenny on the A40. From South Wales, travel via Cardiff and Merthyr Tydfil on the A470, or if you are coming from the west, via Ammanford or Llandeilo, take the A40.

If you really want the freedom that public transport gives you, why not travel to the Beacons by train? Abergavenny is well served by trains from Newport and Crewe with easy onward connections to southern and northwest England. From the Midlands, you can get here through Hereford.

Llandeilo and Llandovery in the west are on the magical Heart of Wales Line from Swansea, while Merthyr Tydfil in the south has great connections to Cardiff. Buses can take you from all these points to Brecon, from which local buses or taxis can deliver you to your destination. Coach

FIND OUT MORE

Beacons Bus Hotline: 01873 853254 (May-Sept)
or visit www.visitbreconbeacons.com
❖❖❖
Brecon Mountain Railway: 01685 722988
(Easter to end of Oct) or visit
www.breconmountainrailway.co.uk
Train timetable enquiries: 08457 484950
or visit www.nationalrail.co.uk
❖❖❖
Cycle hire: visit www.cyclebreconbeacons.com
All Wales travel enquiries: 0870 608 2608
or visit www.traveline.org.uk
❖❖❖
For taxi and other travel information, contact
your local information centre or pick up a
National Park Travel Guide. This is also available
online at www.visitbreconbeacons.com

Coed y Rhaeadr, Waterfall Country

11. What to do

"We've been riding for over three hours and we haven't seen a soul all day." This comment from the diary of a horse rider on the Black Mountains section of the 35-mile Three Rivers Ride through the Brecon Beacons National Park is typical.

Three Rivers Ride, Mynydd Illtyd

Once you get away from the main roads and settlements, whether you are riding, walking or cycling, you can feel you have truly got away from it all, and that you have the spectacular scenery of the Beacons all to yourself. The same rider added, after seeing a flock of starlings burst from a tree, "It is one of those moments that leaves you feeling at once intimately connected with the landscape, and yet ephemeral in its presence. For me, that's what a ride like this is all about."

Thousands of other visitors have experienced this fulfilling sense of intimacy with the timeless landscape of the Beacons by leaving their cars behind and getting out to enjoy the scenery at first hand. It really is the best way to appreciate the varied landscape and wildlife of the National Park.

And the Beacons are particularly well blessed with walking and riding opportunities, including no less than three long distance footpaths. The 100-mile (161km) Beacons Way runs the length of the National Park from Abergavenny to Llangadog; Offa's Dyke Path National Trail (see box) traverses the eastern boundary of the Park, and the 55-mile (93km) Taff Trail links the capital city of Cardiff to Brecon, and has a circular option for walkers around the area of the Central Beacons.

To make it even easier, an increasing number of companies now offer a baggage-carrying service for walkers on the Beacons Way, a walk which was the brainchild of the late Brecon Beacons Park Society Secretary John Sansom, working in conjunction with Arwel Michael and Chris Barber. The Beacons Way is a route for serious walkers, and can be split up into eight day-long walks, linked to local accommodation. An illustrated guidebook is available from Information Centres and bookshops.

The National Park Authority also publishes a series of reasonably priced waterproof walk cards describing purely local walks. Typical is the one describing the delightful nine-mile ascent from Abergavenny to the 1,955ft (596m) summit of the Sugar Loaf (Pen-y-Fal). The walk passes through Deri Fach wood and then across the open mountainside to the summit, with its spectacular views west to the flat-topped summits of the Central Beacons, east to the limestone crags of Cerrigcalch, north to the Black Mountains and Hatterall Hill, and south to Blorenge across the pastoral Usk Valley. The descent is via Mynydd Llanwenarth and then through the beautiful beech woods of St Mary's Vale back to Abergavenny.

The new *Wildlife Walks* booklet can be used to guide you and the family to a dozen wonderful nature reserves brimming with wildlife within the National Park. All the walks are less than two hours in length and many take less than an hour, so they are eminently suitable for families with small children. They include such beautiful spots as Llangors Lake, Mynydd Illtyd, Craig Cerrig-gleisiad NNR, the waterfalls of the Neath Valley, and the Carreg Cennen woodlands near Llandeilo.

A more recent addition to the Park's large range of walking literature are the Geotrails, which provide an easy-to-follow introduction to the rocks and minerals of the National Park. Linked to the Fforest Fawr Geopark (Parc Daearegol Fforest Fawr), designated by UNESCO in 2005, they are designed to be understood and enjoyed by the average visitor.

Horse riders are really spoilt for choice because, in addition to the British Horse Society's Three Rivers Ride, which snakes across the Park between Hay Bluff and Libanus and is part of the National Bridleways Network, the National Park has over 600 miles of bridle paths and tracks. Most treks and hacks are guided, but if you are a more experienced rider and want to set off on your own, each centre will have suggested routes when you hire your horse.

Several long-distance horse riding routes are being developed on the Epynt, in Crychan Fforest and at Torfaen. The Epynt Way links to the Crychan Fforest and the Three Rivers Ride. There are plenty of farms, pubs and small hotels

Wildlife Walk

Taff Trail

Mountains. There really is something for everybody here, with even Herbal Healing and Gardener's Paradise rides in the Tywi Valley pack, whilst Sarn Helen and the Roman Roads and Llanthony Priory and the Gospel Pass rides are included in the Brecon pack.

There is also a new series of walks, cycle routes and horse riding routes called Loops and Links to the south of the National Park associated with the Taff Trail and created by the Groundwork Trust. The National Park also runs an extensive programme of guided walks, which are detailed in its *Walks and Events* guide or from staff at any information centre.

Last but not least, there are plenty of easy routes for those with limited mobility, families with pushchairs and wheel-chair users. Contact an information centre or purchase a copy of the National Park Authority's guide, *Places to Visit with Easier Access*.

And when you get back from your walk or ride, don't forget to reward yourself with a pint or a meal in the local pub or restaurant. There's no better way to finish off a memorable day spent out of doors enjoying the fabulous scenery of the Beacons.

willing to put up both horse and rider along the route and several centres will provide guides, horses and horse boxes for riders wanting a longer challenge.

An increasingly popular way of seeing the National Park is by bike, particularly mountain bike. And there's no more environmentally friendly way to explore the National Park. Cycling has the dual advantages of being both fun and healthy, and the magnificent mountain scenery can never look better than from the saddle of a bike.

Whether you want to traverse the high mountains, cruise through the passes, hop easily from pub to pub or just amuse the kids on a sunny Sunday afternoon, there's something here for everybody, and biking is a great way to escape the stresses and strain of everyday life. You can cruise easily along quiet country lanes, follow traffic-free trails through beautiful wooded valleys or while away a few memorable hours enjoying the timeless tranquillity of some sections of the towpath of Brecon and Monmouthshire Canal.

The National Park's *Brecon* and *Tywi Valley Cycle Breaks* packs include 10 rides in and around the National Park, varying in difficulty from easy family riding along the canalside to a two-day tour of the mountains and valleys of the Black

OFFA'S DYKE PATH

Speaking at the annual general meeting of the Offa's Dyke Path Association a few years ago, its president Lord Sandford described it as: "Not the oldest, nor the longest, but the best." The 177-mile Offa's Dyke long distance footpath – now described as a National Trail – was the brainchild of local rambler and WEA tutor Frank Noble of Knighton, who had been inspired by the work of archaeologist Sir Cyril Fox. The path, which follows the line of King Offa of Mercia's bound-ary for over 60 miles, was officially opened by Everest hero Lord John Hunt of Llanfair Waterdine in 1971.

Dan yr Ogof © GEOPICTURES.NET

12. Where to Go

Although undoubtedly the best way to enjoy the Brecon Beacons National Park is in the great outdoors, there are plenty of other places to go and things to do on those rainy days when heading for the hills may not seem quite so appealing.

The area of the Beacons is rich in fabulous, fairy-tale castles, deep showcaves with amazing underground formations, and fascinating museums to enthral both young and old. You can also discover the area's past by visiting ancient hillforts and burial mounds, Roman roads and lively heritage centres. Or you can enjoy the **Brecon Mountain Railway** – a narrow gauge steam railway which takes you from Merthyr Tydfil and the South Wales valleys into the foothills of the Beacons; the **National Showcaves Centre for Wales** at Dan yr Ogof (which also has its own dinosaur park); **Craig-y-nos Country Park**, the only one within the National Park, in the Upper Tawe Valley. Add to those a multitude of quaint country towns, villages and churches and there's something for everyone.

If history is your thing you must make time to visit **Carreg Cennen Castle**, surely one of the most spectacularly-sited in Britain. It stands on a sheer limestone crag rising 300 feet above the Cennen Valley and has magnificent views of the Black Mountain. The existing stronghold of Carreg Cennen dates from the thirteenth century and stands on the site of even earlier fortifications. Don't miss the 200-foot long underground tunnel reached from inside the castle walls,

Nationl Showcaves Centre for Wales, Dan yr Ogof © GEOPICTURES.NET

Dinosaur Park, Dan yr Ogof © GEOPICTURES.NET

Carreg Cennen Castle CADW. CROWN COPYRIGHT

which burrows through the face of the crag. Nearby on the outskirts of Llandeilo in landscaped parklands stands **Dinefwr Castle,** the ancestral home and royal seat of the Rhys family.

Tretower Castle and Court, near Crickhowell, is really a castle within a castle. The twelfth century shell keep is enclosed by the walls of Picard's later thirteenth century cylindrical tower. Tretower really amounts to a history lesson in the defensive architecture of the English-Welsh Borders, because it stands on the site of an earlier, eleventh century motte and bailey. Nearby is Tretower Court, built in the fourteenth century as a fortified manor house when the threat of invasion had passed.

To the south of the National Park is the Blaenavon World Heritage Site, which bears eloquent testimony to the prominence of South Wales as the world's major producer of iron and coal during the nineteenth century. All the necessary elements can be seen in this microcosm of the industry, including coal and ore mines, quarries, a primitive railway system, furnaces, the homes of workers and the entire social infrastructure of their community. This hub of the Industrial Revolution is being redeveloped fast, with many restored reminders of the town's former status. The mighty iron foundry, which once formed the cutting edge of twentieth century technology, is now being lovingly restored and interpreted.

And at nearby **Big Pit**, you can actually go down a coal mine guided by men who until relatively recently earned their living at the underground hell of the coalface. Using just a bit of imagination, you can still see these now-quiet hillsides teeming with the activities of men, women, children and horses, and explore the rapidly-healing landscape which is still scarred with the remains of its industrial past.

The first major communications systems of the industrial era were the canals, and the **Brecon and Monmouthshire**

Tretower Castle CADW. CROWN COPYRIGHT

Canal, completed in 1812 and linking Brecon with Newport, still winds through the National Park. Today, however, it is a quiet haven through which you can walk along the towpath, take a day trip or hire a narrow boat for a peaceful holiday. The first two miles of the Taff Trail cycling route from Brecon also utilises the canal towpath.

A host of visitor centres and museums tell the story of the Beacons through the ages. Good examples include the **St Mary's Cathedral Heritage Centre** and **South Wales Borderers' Museum** at Brecon, and the **Canal Visitor Centre** at Govilon or the **Llandovery Heritage Centre**. Other interesting museums include **Brecknock Museum** at Brecon; **Cyfartha Castle, Museum and Art Gallery** at Merthyr Tydfil, and **Abergavenny Museum**, which is set within the grounds of the town's ruined Norman castle.

Abergavenny and Brecon have high quality theatres offering an impressive array of drama, concerts and dance. The two-screen cinema in Brecon carries all the mainstream films and has a monthly film club. Several towns have leisure centres, and the one at Brecon also offers 10-pin bowling in addition to a swimming pool, a gym and squash courts.

Hay-on-Wye book town

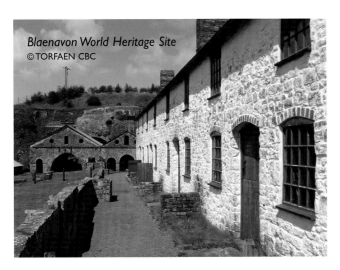

Blaenavon World Heritage Site
© TORFAEN CBC

For the very young there are two indoor play barns – one at Brynich on the outskirts of Brecon and the other at Cantref, incorporating an adventure farm. The Multi Activity Centre at Llangors also has a range of indoor and outdoor activities for all the family from climbing to sailing through the air along wires high above the ground. The Forestry Commission's Garwnant Visitor Centre, just five miles north of Merthyr Tydfil, provides an ideal place to 'play in the woods' with a fantastic ropes course for the adventurous, as well as woodland walking trails, a family cycle route and a toddlers' play area.

Another good rainy day alternative is a visit to **Hay-on-Wye**, otherwise known as 'the **Town of Books**.' Here is the

biggest collection of second-hand bookshops in Britain, with an estimated one million titles for sale in over 30 shops in the little market town at the foot of the Black Mountains. Hay really has become a booklovers' paradise ever since the eccentric local entrepreneur, Richard Booth of Hay Castle, started the speciality. Every spring Hay plays host to the Hay Festival of Literature, attracting top authors from all over the world.

Visiting gardens has become a major visitor destination in recent years, and visitors to the National Park are lucky to have two of the finest botanical gardens in the country within easy day-trip distance. **The National Botanic Garden of Wales** at Llanarthne, midway between Cross Hands and Carmarthen, was the first national botanic garden to be created in Britain this century. Since then, it has developed into one of the most fascinating gardens in the UK, it has become the most visited garden in Wales, and was recently voted the Number One "Wonder of Wales" by the local daily newspaper. It also does valuable conservation work in helping to protect and propagate some of the rarest plants in the world.

Beautifully set in the lovely Tywi Valley, **Aberglasney House** at Llangathen, a few miles west of Llandeilo, also boasts another of the finest gardens in Wales. **Aberglasney Gardens** have been an inspiration to poets such as owner John Dyer since the fifteenth century. The story of Aberglasney really starts with John's father Robert Dyer, a successful Carmarthen lawyer who purchased the house in 1710. It was Dyer who gave the house its current whitewashed Queen Anne style façade.

A good starting point for any exploration of the National Park and what there is to do and see is the National Park's own purpose-built **Visitor Centre** at Libanus, south west of Brecon off the A470. Here you can find out more about the whole of the National Park, its history and its people, through lively events and displays. There is

National Botanic Gardens of Wales © NBG of W

also an excellent restaurant/teashop, serving home-made local produce.

For more information of things to see and do, get your copy of the *Brecon Beacons National Park Visitor Guide*. This full colour, 72-page booklet gives information on everything from walking to the World Heritage Site, and also has details of accommodation in the area. It is widely available at visitor centres throughout the National Park.

Aberglasney Gardens and House © ABERGLASNEY

TO MARKET, TO MARKET...

Markets and fairs are fascinating places in which to browse, chat and experience local life. They can also throw up some real bargains. Farmers' markets are the increasingly popular occasions where you can meet the actual people who grow the food you are buying – so you know it is locally produced. Arts, crafts and antique fairs are becoming a real speciality of the area and the list below tells you where and when to visit them.

Retail Markets
Tuesday: Abergavenny and Brecon
Thursday: Crickhowell and Hay-on-Wye
Friday: Brecon and Llandeilo

Farmers' Markets
Abergavenny: fourth Thursday of each month
Brecon: second Saturday of each month

Antique and Collectors' Fairs
Abergavenny: third Saturday of each month
Brecon: last Saturday of each month

Craft Fairs
Abergavenny: second Saturday of each month
Brecon: third Saturday of each month

Talybont Reservoir

13. Gazetteer of Towns and Villages

Abergavenny (Y Fenni)

Abergavenny is the traditional gateway to South Wales and to the Brecon Beacons National Park. The Sugar Loaf, Blorenge and Skirrid are right on the edge of town making you feel you are right in the heart of the mountains, but not hemmed in by them. The town's history goes back to the Roman fort of *Gobannivm* established in 57 or 58 AD. However, the real birth of the town was during the Norman conquest of Wales in the late eleventh century, and the impressive castle ruins, now home to a fascinating museum, still dominate the Usk Valley a short walk from the town centre. In the seventeenth and eighteenth centuries, flannel weaving, tanning and goat-hair wig making were important industries, and by the end of the eighteenth century, in the wake of the Industrial Revolution, many of the old Tudor houses were refurbished with fashionable Georgian frontages. The Abergavenny of the nineteenth century was a bustling cultural centre and holds an important place in Welsh literary and cultural history. The town began to expand once more with the coming of the railways in the middle of the 1850s. Many of the interesting features of the old town, such as fireplaces, doors, oak panelling and windows, are now on display in the Abergavenny Museum, while the Abergavenny Food Festival in September has gained a national reputation. Abergavenny is well served by trains from Newport and Manchester, with easy connections from England and South Wales.

Abergavenny Museum

Abergavenny

Bethlehem

Bethlehem is a tiny farming village on the hillside south of Llangadog, overlooking the River Tywi. Because of its biblical name, the post office is renowned for franking cards at Christmas time, and each year thousands of people send their cards to be stamped with the Bethlehem postmark. Behind the village on the bracken-covered hillside is the site of a Bronze Age burial cairn and the impressive Iron Age hillfort of Garn Goch, said to be one of the largest in Europe.

Blaenavon (Blaenafon)

Blaenavon is the best preserved example of a traditional South Wales iron-making town. It is probably unique in Europe in possessing one of the best preserved late eighteenth and early nineteenth century ironworks in the world and a mine, now a museum, which provides underground tours. Blaenavon was designated an Industrial Landscape World Heritage Site in 2000 in recognition of its extraordinary past and as the world example of the growth of the coke-fuelled iron industry, alongside Ironbridge in Shropshire. Just under half of the Blaenavon World Heritage Site lies within the boundaries of the National Park.

Brecon (Aberhonddu)

Historic Brecon is the bustling 'capital' and headquarters of the National Park Authority. Narrow compact streets, Georgian facades and the restored canal basin tell tales of times gone by, while the twelfth century cathedral, South Wales Borderers Military Museum, and Brecknock Museum and Art Gallery, reveal even more of the town's fascinating history. Brecon offers many places to eat and stay, and the monthly Farmers' Market is the biggest in the area. Local butchers and organic and specialist foods are in abundance while more active visitors will enjoy the outdoor shops, bike hire and the Taff Trail cycle path leading from the town. Brecon benefits from a wide range of shops, evening entertainment and places to stay, and with a professional theatre and independent cinema, pubs and restaurants and a leisure centre for rainy days, there's always something to do in this pleasant market town.

Welsh hill farmer and sheepdog, near Brecon

Brynaman

Brynaman is the western gateway of the Brecon Beacons, leading directly into the National Park. The village itself stands at the foot of the Black Mountain. Although industry has long gone, some wonderful historical evidence remains from its industrial past. Brynaman grew to service the coal mining industry in the mid 1800s, rapidly growing to accommodate the miners and their families, which is reflected in the architecture of the village and its attractions. The open air swimming pool remains an attraction for locals and tourists alike, as well as the cinema, which was opened in 1926 and paid for by local miners. The swimming pool was the last to be built in south west Wales and still has many of its original features including iron turnstiles and wooden changing huts. The old school has become the new centre of the community, housing the library, café and a heritage display, also exhibiting work from local artists in its gallery, as well as having an arts and craft section. The centre also acts as a Village Information Agency, providing visitor information for attractions in and around the National Park.

Capel Gwynfe

A small village about three miles to the south west of Llangadog, with a picturesque church dating from 1898 and a nineteenth century church hall, recently renovated by the community. The area is mainly agricultural, and its location in the foothills of the Brecon Beacons makes it an ideal starting point for walkers and cyclists. The Beacons Way also passes through the village. Capel Gwynfe was voted Carmarthenshire Village of the Year in 2004, and the village's Spring Show is advertised as a sustainable event, themed, organised and run by the community. There is a spirited wooden carving of three red kites outside the village community centre.

Crickhowell (Crug Hywel)

Crickhowell is a compact and well preserved Georgian town. It has a thirteenth century castle, a seventeenth century bridge (boasting more arches on one side than the other) and just down the road is Tretower Court and

Cwmdu

Castle, an impressive medieval manor house and castle. Crickhowell is easy to get to, has excellent shopping, great accommodation and good food. You can connect to walking trails throughout the Black Mountains, follow the gentle contours of the canal from Llangattock, or just go for a stroll along the Usk in the Riverside Park. Crickhowell is also a mountain biking 'hub' with challenging routes waiting to be explored.

Cwmdu

Cwmdu village lies between the Black Mountains and the Brecon Beacons four miles from Crickhowell. Despite the name (it means 'the black valley'), it is far from gloomy, in fact it is one of the most sheltered and picturesque valleys in the Beacons. From the village there is access to the many footpaths which lead up into the hills. A scenic mountain route leads you to Llangors Lake for other activities such as riding and hang gliding.

Defynnog

The fifteenth century church of St Cynog houses an early medieval inscribed stone and Celtic font and holy water stoup. Near the church is the former vicarage (c.1721) and a row of nineteenth century estate cottages. The Old School Art Gallery & Craft Centre displaying the work of local creators is also worth a browse, and offers the opportunity to sit down with a cake and coffee in the Victorian tea rooms.

Glasbury-on-Wye

Glasbury is beautifully situated on the River Wye with the impressive backdrop of the Black Mountain, 12 miles from Brecon and 28 miles from the nearest railway station at Hereford. The riverside meadows and common land are ideal for picnics, swimming and boating, and there is a riverside cafe/bistro, a village shop, pub and garage. A canoe centre offers boat hire and tuition if necessary, and other outdoor pursuits centres nearby offer all types of activities, including pony trekking and riding.

Govilon

The village of Govilon in the east lies in the beautiful valley of the River Usk, running through the heart of the National Park. The Monmouthshire and Brecon Canal flows through the village, which is also close to Blaenavon World Heritage Site. The rich history, heritage and environment of the village place it in a unique position. Govilon Post Office also acts as a National Park Village Information Agency.

Hay-on-Wye (Y Gelli)

Hay describes itself as "The Town of Books" with some justification. The town is internationally famous for its 30-plus second-hand bookshops, with over a million books on sale. Hay's speciality as a town for book lovers was started by Richard Booth from what remains of Hay Castle, and a recent spin-off has been the annual Hay Festival of Literature. (see box in Chapter 3). Besides the opportunities for book-browsing, there are high quality bistros and restaurants and you can explore a range of galleries, clothing and crafts shops. Hay is on the edge of the Black Mountains and the Offa's Dyke National Trail runs through the town. It makes a great base for walkers or for anyone wanting to use the Wye for canoeing or fishing. Or you can take a stroll along the river or catch the Offa's Dyke Flyer bus to Hay Bluff to enjoy spectacular views.

Libanus

Libanus is a small village about five miles south west of Brecon, standing at the base of the Beacons and with spectacular views of the reigning summit of Pen y Fan. It is possible to walk onto the mountains straight from the village, and is a perfect location for those wishing to explore the Central Beacons. The National Park Visitor Centre is situated within two miles of Libanus, where there are also spectacular views of the Beacons and you can discover more about the heritage of the National Park. The centre is situated on Mynydd Illtyd, a large common where sheep and wild ponies graze. Nearby is a Bronze Age burial cairn, and a Roman road across the middle of the common heads towards Sennybridge. Libanus is approximately one hour from Cardiff, Swansea and the Gower Coast. Merthyr Tydfil, the nearest railway station, is 15 miles away, and it is on the bus route between Merthyr and Brecon.

Llandeilo

Llandeilo is an ancient market town in a beautiful setting. Dinefwr Castle stands on the edge of the town, while nearby Carreg Cennen must be the most spectacular castle in Wales, sited on top of steep limestone cliffs with woodland walks and a great teashop. Nearby Aberglasney Gardens is a garden lost in time while the National Botanic Garden of Wales is also close at hand. Antiques, music, good food and high quality shops all add up to a very Welsh experience.

Llandeilo

its famous aqueduct over the river, are both nearby. Llanfrynach is situated in the foothills of the Beacons so is another ideal location for walkers. A bus service runs through the village several times a day for those not wishing to drive.

Llangadog

Situated in the heart of the Towy Valley half way between Llandeilo and Llandovery, Llangadog is a village with stunning views towards the Black Mountain and a population of about 1000 people. The village is well served by places to stay, eat and drink. The church of St Cadog, renowned for its beautiful stained glass windows, stands on the site of a medieval Celtic Christian community. Nearby is the Coed Pen Arthur Forest Park, where a network of forest roads and easy footpaths provide opportunities for circular walks, criss-crossing the River Meilwch.

Llanthony

Set in the remote Vale of Ewyas, the twelfth century priory of Llanthony is one of the most romantic ruins in Wales. The priory, now in the care of Cadw, rather incongruously incorporates a small hotel in its ruins, but it is the ruined arcade of pointed Early English-style arches framing the Black Mountains behind which catches most attention.

Llangors

Llangors is a lovely village with a beautiful fifteenth century parish church. It is a centre for all kinds of outdoor activities, with easy access to the mountains. The one and a half mile long and half-mile wide lake is a protected wildlife site, designated as a Site of Special Scientific Interest (SSSI), and is also home to many water sports with boats available for hire and a National Park Village Information Agency within the Lakeside shop. It also features a Dark Age crannog (a man-made island settlement), and a reconstruction shows what it must once have looked like. Pony trekking, indoor climbing and high wire courses are all available locally.

Llandovery (Llanymddyfri)

Llandovery is well placed as a base for the west of the National Park on the beautiful Heart of Wales railway line. It was formerly a major drovers' town and in those days it could be crammed with 30,000 cattle on their way to London. The Norman castle at Llandovery contains a remarkable memorial to Llewelyn ap Gruffydd Fychan – the Welsh equivalent of the Scottish Braveheart. The Heritage Centre houses innovative displays on local legends such as the Lady of the Lake and the Physicians of Myddfai. Wildlife enthusiasts can visit the nearby Red Kite Feeding Station at Llanddeusant or the RSPB's Dinas Reserve.

Llanfrynach

Llanfrynach two and a half miles south-east of Brecon is small and quiet with only one pub, which provides excellent food in the bar and restaurant. In the centre of the village is the attractive parish church, surrounded by a large churchyard and some fine houses. The tower was rebuilt in 1855. In 1783, a Roman villa was discovered west of the village, complete with bathhouse and mosaics. The River Usk and the Monmouthshire and Brecon Canal, with

Llangynidr

Llangynidr is an unusual village because it has both the Brecon and Monmouthshire Canal and the River Usk running through it. On the canal, brightly-painted boats leisurely pass by or wait their turn to pass through the five locks which lift the canal 50ft (15.2m) in three-quarters of a mile (1.2km). The River Usk is famous for its excellent trout and salmon fishing (fishing can be arranged) and it runs through some exceptionally beautiful stretches here, with rocks and rapids. The single lane bridge into the village over the river is narrow and heavily buttressed. The village itself is an excellent location for exploring the National Park, and there is a choice of pubs, restaurants and shops. Nearby attractions include Talybont Reservoir and the fascinating Tretower Court and Castle historic house. Llangynidr is on the bus route mid-way between Abergavenny and Brecon, approximately 12 miles from Abergavenny, which is the nearest railway station.

Merthyr Tydfil

Merthyr Tydfil, in the northern part of the Taff Valley, gets its name from Tydful, the daughter of Brychan, Prince of Brycheiniog, who was slain by marauding Picts in the fifth century. The site where she was killed became known as Martyr Tudfyl (now Merthyr Tydfil). The early eighteenth century saw the establishment of the huge iron works complexes, which made Merthyr the Iron Capital of the World. The past 20 years have seen a remarkable transformation with considerable reclamation work creating many environmental improvements. Situated on the southern boundary of the National Park, Merthyr Tydfil is the perfect centre for a wide range of activities and attractions. Walkers will find an endless choice of both challenging and gentler routes including the long distance Taff Trail, which links the capital city of Cardiff to the historic market town of Brecon. Within Merthyr itself, there are a variety of local heritage trails which highlight the town's historic sites and places of interest. Set in beautiful parkland on the edge of the National Park is the Cyfartha Castle Museum and Art Gallery. Ironmaster William Crawshay commissioned its building in 1824, and this grand castellated mansion now houses extensive collections of fine and decorative art.

Myddfai

The small parish of Myddfai is situated at the foot of Mynydd Myddfai and the Black Mountain. At the centre of the village is the ancient parish church of St. Michael's, which has probably been the site of Christian worship for a thousand years. The treasures of the church include the parish registers dating back to 1653. Several periods of major restoration and repair have most recently included re-roofing and the redecoration of the interior in 1992. Myddfai was also the home of the farmer who fell in love with and married the fairy lady of Llyn y Fan Fach (see Chapter 8, Legends, culture and customs) and later the famous Meddygon Myddfai, or the Physicians of Myddfai.

Myddfai Church

Pontneddfechan

Pontneddfechan was once the scene of great industrial activity. Limestone was quarried from the Dinas Rock for the production of lime for agriculture, building and road metalling, while the Gunpowder Works alongside the river Mellte was the only example of its kind in Wales. The gunpowder was principally for use in coal mines and quarries, including the slate quarries of Snowdonia. Although largely in ruins today, visitors can still see some massive stonework and the remains of many buildings. Silica rock or quartzite was also mined in the Pontneddfechan area from the late eighteenth century up until 1964. It is a hard rock with a very high melting point and was used for producing high quality fire-bricks. The remains of the old levels and tramways can also still be seen. Today visitors come to Pontneddfechan to explore its fascinating industrial heritage and visit Fforest Fawr Geopark and the 'Waterfall Country'.

Sennybridge (Pontsenni)

Sennybridge is a sheep and cattle market town eight miles west of Brecon on the Llandovery road. It is relatively young compared to its neighbours Defynnog and Trecastell, because in 1820, Sennybridge didn't exist. It was the coming of the Neath-Brecon railway in the late 1860's which saw the importance and size of the village increase to such an extent that it began to overtake Trecastell as the centre of the community. Today it perhaps is best-known for its Army Camp, but there are also four pubs, a resource centre, a post office and various shops. Sennybridge Spar Shop doubles as a National Park Village Information Agency, and the village is also a mountain biking 'hub.' Castell Du, across the Senni, was a fourteenth century keep where offenders caught hunting in Fforest Fawr were imprisoned.

Talgarth

The small and ancient market town of Talgarth stands beneath the Black Mountains, and forms an excellent gateway to them for hill walking or mountain biking. Close by are two nature reserves, Park Wood and Pwll-y-Wrach, featured in the National Park's Wildlife Walks booklet. The fourteenth century Pele Tower in the town square is now the Tourist Information Centre. The religious settlement which Hywel Harris (the founder of Welsh Methodism) set up in nearby Trefeca still survives as a college and museum. Gentle woodland walking can be found in nearby Park Wood.

Talgarth

Pontneddfechan

Talybont-on-Usk

Pretty Talybont lies below the Central Beacons between the Usk and the Brecon and Monmouthshire Canal. It is a great place for hill walkers, cyclists and those wanting interesting strolls with an excellent range of pubs serving food to suit all pockets. There is a National Park Village Information Agency at the Post Office and Stores. The Taff Trail and Brinore Tramroad offer historic cycling and walking routes up into the mountains. If you want a quiet stroll though, the Henry Vaughan walk takes you around the nearby country-side introducing you to the eighteenth century poet who lived nearby. Talybont Reservoir offers bird-watching, trout fishing and an easier one-mile walk around the mini 'waterfalls area' at Blaen y Glyn.

Trecastle

The village of Trecastle is situated on the A40 between Brecon and Llandovery, and was once an old coaching village on the route from Gloucester to Llandovery. Evidence for this can still be seen in the old coaching inns which provided accommodation for travellers. The minor road adjacent to one of the old inns, the Castle Hotel, leads to the Usk Reservoir, and the scenic route to Llanddeusant with its splendid views of the Carmarthen Fans. Trecastle is named after an early twelfth century motte and bailey fortification built by Bernard de Neufmarche, half-brother of William the Conqueror. It is the largest example of a motte and bailey castle in the National Park. Near the village can be found the site of Y Pigwn – an important Roman military overnight marching camp. Near the appropriately named hamlet of Halfway located between Trecastle and Llandovery there is an obelisk on the roadside which was 'erected as a caution to keep from intoxication' and commemorates a coach full of passengers which crashed down into the adjoining river in 1835.

Tretower

Tretower village boasts a Norman tower, the remains of a motte and bailey castle, and next to this a fascinating medieval manor house with fortifications and reconstructed medieval garden. Open air theatre performances are staged in the courtyard during the summer season. This is a popular film location, and an audio-guide can be hired at the house, which takes you through the history of the castle and house, pointing out details and providing information which may otherwise be missed. Tretower is three miles from Crickhowell and 11 miles from Brecon.

Ystradfellte

The historic village of Ystradfellte is set in the beautiful Mellte Valley, surrounded by heather-covered moors and rich farmland. The Mellte River has cut down through the hard limestone to create spectacular wooded gorges, and Ystradfellte makes a good base from which to explore the waterfalls of the Hepste and Mellte rivers between the village and Pontneddfechan. Perhaps the most impressive is Sgwd yr Eira (Fall of Snow), which once allowed the careful explorer to walk behind it, but the natural processes which helped create it are now making the overhanging rocks unstable, and access to the waterfall is restricted from time to time to allow such problems to be dealt with (either naturally or through man's intervention) to make it safe again. Much of the present parish church of St. Mary at Ystradfellte was constructed by Cistercian monks at the end of the twelfth century. The plain Norman chancel, being slightly offset and of simple masonry, is typical of early Cistercian churches.

Ystradgynlais

Ystradgynlais is flanked by mountains – The Drum, Cribarth, also known as The Sleeping Giant, Farteg and Mynydd Du – and bisected by the Tawe River on its way to the sea at Swansea. An excellent road connects the area to the M4 motorway 12 miles down the valley. Standing Stones such as Maen Llia and Maen Madog, bones and other artefacts attest to early human occupation. An ancient stone circle, Cerrig Duon, with its attendant standing stone, Maen Mawr, alongside the young Tawe River, are aligned to a row of stones known as the Saith Maen or Seven Stones which lies on top of Cribarth. The parish church of Ystradgynlais, St. Cynog's, rebuilt in 1865, is the latest of a succession of churches believed to extend back to the sixth century. It is probable that the earliest church on the site was associated with, or founded by, Cynog, son of the Irish king Brychan who lent his name to Brycheiniog or Brecknock, one of the old kingdoms, and later counties incorporated into the present county of Powys. Fragments of early Christian memorial stones are incorporated into the fabric of the building, and ancient yew trees stand in the surrounding churchyard.

Govilon Wharf, Monmouthshire & Brecon Canal

Walkers, Mynydd Illtyd Common

14. The National Park Today

The 50th anniversary of the National Park is a time for celebration of this beautiful, dynamic landscape and what it means to the people who live, work and visit here. But it is also a time of reflection and planning for the future. What do we want the National Park to look like and mean to us in another 50 years time?

Current thinking places much emphasis on global warming and the long-term effects which climate change will bring to us all. The National Park Authority is striving to address this important issue in everything it does, from the development and implementation of its National Park Management Plan and Local Development Plan, to influencing those around us to make the small individual changes in lifestyle which are needed to sustain the way of life we hold so dear.

The National Park Authority cannot do this alone, and it works closely with many partner organisations to achieve these aims, among them the National Trust, the Forestry Commission and the nine Unitary Authorities which fall within the National Park boundary.

Twenty-four members make up the National Park Authority, which has been a free-standing, special purpose authority within local government, since 1996. Sixteen of the members are county councillors, appointed by the local constituent Unitary Authorities, and eight are appointed by the Welsh Assembly Government, through a competitive application process.

Seventy-five percent of the Authority's net budget is directly funded by the Welsh Assembly, and the Unitary Authorities are levied for the remaining quarter. Additional funding comes from grants and income from the services and facilities provided for the public in the form of planning fees, the sale of publications and refreshments at visitor centres, car parking fees and educational visits. All are important in helping to increase the amount of wide-ranging, varied work which the Authority undertakes for the long-term benefit of all.

With an annual budget of around £6 million, the Authority strives to:-

- enhance the enjoyment and understanding of those who live in and visit the National Park through its information and interpretation services
- maintain and improve access along the 1,983km (1,232 miles) of public rights of way which run through the Park
- support local community sustainable development initiatives
- conserve the landscape and habitats it supports for the well-being and enjoyment of generations to come.
- ensure building developments are sensitively and sustainably designed, with provision of affordable homes for local people.

Useful Addresses

Brecon Beacons National Park Authority
Plas y Ffynonn
Cambrian Way
Brecon
Powys LD3 7HP
Tel: 01874 624437
Website: www.breconbeacons.org
Email: enquiries@breaconbeacons.org

Cadw
Welsh Assembly Government Buildings
Plas Carew
Unit 5/7 Cefn Coed
Parc Nantgarw
Cardiff CF15 7QQ
Tel: 01443 33 6000
Website: www.cadw.wales.gov.uk
Email: cadw@wales.gsi.gov.uk

Brecknock Wildlife Trust
Lion House
Bethel Square
Brecon
Powys LD3 7AY.
Tel: 01874 625708
Website:
www.brecknockwildlifetrust.org.uk
Email: brecknockwt@cix.xo.uk

Campaign for the
Protection of Rural Wales
Ty Gwyn
31 High Street
Welshpool
Powys SY21 7YD
Website: www.cprw.org.uk
Tel: 01938 552525 or 01938 556212
Email: www.cprw.org.uk

Countryside Council for Wales
Cantref Court
Brecon Road
Abergavenny
Powys NP7 7AX
Tel: 01873 737000
Website: www.ccw.gov.uk
Email: cardiffreception@ccw.gov.uk

Forestry Commission Wales
Victoria House
Victoria Terrace
Aberystwyth
Ceredigion
SY23 2DQ
Tel: 0845 604 0845
Website: www.forestry.gov.uk

Welsh Water
Plas y Ffynnon
Cambrian Way
Brecon
Powys LD3 7HP
Email: enquiries@dwrcymru.com

Brecon Beacons Tourism Association
Glynmeddig
Pentrefelin
Sennybridge
Powys LD3 8UA
Tel: 01874 638949
Website: www.getactive-beacons.co.uk
Email: enquiries@getactive-beacons.co.uk

Wales Tourist Board
Brunel House
2 Fitzalan Road
Cardiff CF24 0UY
Tel: 08708 300 306
Website: www.visitwales.com
Email: info@visitwales.co.uk

Council for National Parks
6-7 Barnard Mews
London SW11 1QU
Tel: 020 7924 4077
Website: www.cnp.org.uk
Email: info@cnp.org.uk

Maps
Ordnance Survey Explorer Maps (1:25,000)
OL12 Brecon Beacons National Park, Western & Central Areas
OL13 Brecon Beacons National Park, Eastern Area